TEAMMATES

A Situational IT-com

Williams Rajakumar

Chennai • Bangalore

CLEVER FOX PUBLISHING
Chennai, India

Published by CLEVER FOX PUBLISHING 2023
Copyright © Williams Rajakumar 2023

All Rights Reserved.
ISBN: 978-93-56485-00-6

This book has been published with all reasonable efforts taken to make the material error-free after the consent of the author. No part of this book shall be used, reproduced in any manner whatsoever without written permission from the author, except in the case of brief quotations embodied in critical articles and reviews.

The Author of this book is solely responsible and liable for its content including but not limited to the views, representations, descriptions, statements, information, opinions and references ["Content"]. The Content of this book shall not constitute or be construed or deemed to reflect the opinion or expression of the Publisher or Editor. Neither the Publisher nor Editor endorse or approve the Content of this book or guarantee the reliability, accuracy or completeness of the Content published herein and do not make any representations or warranties of any kind, express or implied, including but not limited to the implied warranties of merchantability, fitness for a particular purpose. The Publisher and Editor shall not be liable whatsoever for any errors, omissions, whether such errors or omissions result from negligence, accident, or any other cause or claims for loss or damages of any kind, including without limitation, indirect or consequential loss or damage arising out of use, inability to use, or about the reliability, accuracy or sufficiency of the information contained in this book.

WILLIAMS RAJAKUMAR

Williams Rajakumar is a biology specimen, engineered in chemical, coded in an IT firm, screwed up with an MBA, analyzed self in a data service firm and now to add more seriousness to life, took up Stand-up comedy and writing.

He can be contacted at williamsch53@gmail.com

DEDICATED TO MY SON RACHIN

ACKNOWLEDGEMENTS

I would like to express my sincere gratitude to my Dad Mr.Rajakumar, for guiding me through all obstacles and providing me with the best education possible despite all odds. He is an ex-servicemen and one could literally hear 'left right left' when he walks, as it looks like performing march past. He desperately wanted to land me in a secure white collar job, but I signaled 'left' and took 'right' to his dismay.

My Mom Mrs.Dhanalakshmi, for pouring out immense love, care and rasam. I firmly believe I have got the gene of writing from her for 2 reasons. Firstly, she inks her emotions. Secondly, i am pretty sure it's not from my dad

My studious sister Dr.Jennifer, for mercilessly searching the flunked papers from my school bag and handing it over to my dad with utmost satisfaction. Now the same hands are excited to pick up and read my book

My wife Mrs.Sathya, for making my life feel complete. Had she not come into my life, I wouldn't be pursuing my passion and roasting my well wishers here, so I thank my father-in-law Mr.MeenakshiSundaram and mother-in-law Mrs.Shanthi for handing over their heartache to me oops! sweetheart to me and trusting us in all our major decisions. She helped me to beat the weekday blues and now every morning feels like weekend hues

This book is available in paperback and kindle version but Ramkumar is, and will be the only person to have heard the audio version which was forcefully narrated to him by me. His constant motivation, honest review and valuable inputs helped me complete this book. He picked the title "Teammates" among the few options I shared, which I froze without any second opinion, as none dared to read the book.

Ashwanth Abraham for giving valuable suggestions when sought for support during the initial phase of writing and later he blocked my number.

It sounds uplifting to read the quote 'Don't judge the book by its cover' but research said 'Many judge the book by its cover', so I approached my artistic friend Stalinkumar for designing this beautiful cover. If you are reading this now, then he has succeeded

Mervyn Rosario, for inspiring me to quit my white collar job, which he never wants to be known for, especially to my family

CONTENTS

CHAPTER 1 – IT STORE AND ESCALATION IN CAFETERIA	1
CHAPTER 2 - EFFORT & CRUSH TRACKER	27
CHAPTER 3 – BEST OUTFIT AND SECURITY ANNA	45
CHAPTER 4 – BIRTHDAY AND BIRTH CHART	58
CHAPTER 5 - WATER BOTTLE AND BOTTLENECK SITUATION	80
CHAPTER 6 – BAY DECORATION AND CRITICAL PRIORITY ISSUE	94
CHAPTER 7 – DIM SPOT AND ROOMIES	117
CHAPTER 8 – FRIGHT FRIDAY AND COOL TRANSFER	133
CHAPTER 9 – TAX FILING AND HEART BLOCKS	158
CHAPTER 10 – FAREWELL AND FRESHERS	173

theme park, prefers wearing checked casual shirts, plain cotton pants and doesn't tuck in except for client meeting.

As he sensed that the admin was looking at him, he then turned and asked 'It's obvious that this is an infrared sensor, I am not going to ask you about that, but do you know the frequency?'

'The door would open when swiped, that's all I know about it,' said the admin with nil expression.

'No curiosity,' disappointed Chocku, swiped the access and got inside.

Vinoth and Chocku greet each other. Vinoth knew that Chocku was supposed to meet a bride's family last weekend and he is also aware that the bridal search has been going on for the last 3 years.

'How did the bride visit go?' asked Vinoth in excitement.

'Bride visit went well but pity that the bridegroom visit didn't go as expected,' sympathised Chocku.

Vinoth was confused and asked 'I can't get you. You mean, you went to see a bride groom too? Had you lost hope in finding a bride?' asked in suspicion.

'No, we liked the bride but the bridegroom's family didn't like us.'

'Oh! sorry about that, even, I was in such a situation before. I would feel bad when I get rejected and someday it just happens. Feeling dejected, I only lost some hair strands. Did they mention any reason?'

'Hair should be the reason,' assumed Chocku.

'Really?'

'Nowadays they are more concerned about hair growth than career growth. What can I do about things that's not under my control? Similar to rainfall, the hair whorl intensified into a tornado and rolled throughout my head causing hair fall. It might be because of androgenetic alopecia, telogen effluvium, anagen effluvium, Alopecia areata, Traction alopecia. Who knows?'

'This should have been the reason for rejection and not hair fall,' talked to himself. 'Did you get a chance to speak with the girl?'

'Yeah, we spoke for a few minutes, but it seemed like she was so much into me while I was explaining about astronomy.'

'Now I understand.'

'Understood? But I never spoke to you about astronomy.'

'I said, I understand your problem' and I have a solution for this,' smiled devilishly.

'What is the solution?'

'Solution is the solution.'

Chocku couldn't understand what he was trying to say.

'Cold pressed oil. If you apply it to the roots of your hair and then none can stop your hair from overflowing.'

'Really?' his hair strands stood erect.

'Yes. Even if you try to assign an overflow value, you can't stop it.'

Techie Chocku got trapped by this technical pitch. 'Where can I get it?'

'You can get it in our company.'

'I thought our company was only into software products, when did they venture into organic products? That's a risky move.'

'Not our company product. There is an employee who sells it.'

'Where is he located?'

'In C block, go to the first floor, enter the ODC (Offshore Development Center), take a right and in the corner cubicle you can find him seated facing the window with a Sai Baba statue at his desk.'

Chocku then closed his eyes and ran through his mind visually to locate his place. In C block, I am going to the first floor, entering the ODC, taking a right, corner cubicle, Sai Baba statue. Got up in shock 'It's you?'

'Yes,' leaned back with his legs crossed over. 'IT job is insecure, so I have started to sell some organic products as a back-up business.'

'Fine then I need a bottle.'

'Sure by tomorrow, I will..'

'You will home deliver?' came forward in curiosity

'I will do bay delivery. Rs.150+ no extra charges'

'Do I have any discount?'

'No Discount.'

'Do Jagan know about your side business?' blackmailed Chocku.

Vinoth was worried. Not because he would come to know about his side business but he had sold a bottle to Jagan for Rs.175.

'Ahem! Special price only for you Rs.130 only.'

*

While the business transaction was going on between Chocku and Vinoth, Jagan was stuck outside the ODC as his access card was not working. He waited for someone else to come but lost his patience and made a call to Vinoth.

Jagan has spherical eyes that can squeeze and adjust like a telescope to even monitor the activities of microorganisms,

'*I can hear. I am not deaf,*' translated Aysha.

'Oh! But how come you are able to understand her Aysha?' wondered Vinoth

'I conversed with her in sign language, when I once used to take her snacks.'

'But I didn't come here for snacks,' sheepishly smiled Vinoth.

'Tomorrow I will bring extra snacks for both of you and mail, *sweets at my desk,*' spoke Kavita as the safeguarded snacks reached the digestive juices.

Jagan stopped by and asked, 'Anyone joining me for a 4 mins 30 seconds break? Let's have some Paruppu Vada and Coffee.'

Vinoth gets excited and shouted Ayeee! and cuts the excitement to 'I am coming.'

'Today he is going to be the chutney for his vada,' Kavita told herself.

Aysha nodded 'No' seeing Vinoth.

Vinoth thought that she was jealous of him for raising his hand before she did. Meanwhile, Jagan has started his stopwatch '4 mins 15, 14, 13, 12. Time is running.'

'Running Jagan. Sorry coming Jagan,' left along with him.

Aysha felt there is going to be an escalation today for sure.

They both walked to the canteen and while nearing the ODC exit, Vinoth said, 'Oops I have left the purse in the bay Jagan' but it didn't reach Jagan's ears as the glass door closed once he left first. Vinoth then realized that he should use this phrase only in the canteen.

*

Karthik strode towards the ODC thinking about his career. Though he puts up a positive face in public, deep inside he is sad since there is no driving force for him to work.

Fun effervescing sharp eyes like a bent steel soda bottle. Long nose and appears to have a spacious nasal passage as if he in-hales more oxygen than others. The tip of the nose is pointed and looks like a bow and arrow placed upside down. Thick and boomerang shaped eyebrows like his thoughts that go back and forth. Fit, slim and apt height for his physique. Stubble beard and mustache with thick V shape hair line below the lower lip. Wears a silver cuff bracelet on his right hand. His room is mounted with a dark full hand T shirt or checked shirts with light jeans.

'Good morning akka' (*sister in Tamil*), greeted Karthik while signing the registry note at the admin desk

'Good morning thambi' (*brother in Tamil*).

He then lets out a deep breath while placing the pen on the note unbeknownst to him. This sent a signal to the admin akka though she didn't really notice him sigh everyday but her subconscious mind knew the abnormality.

'You lighten up while you greet but then switch to dull mode as you sign,' asked admin akka.

'Is that how I behave? Maybe because of the work. I feel like something is missing.'

'You might have missed the access card,' she kidded.

He laughed and then realised that he really hadn't brought the card. 'Sorry akka. Give a spare card. I will never forget again.'

'What? Seriously, you don't have it with you?'

Nodded 'Yes.'

'You can get the spare card if you answer me this question'. She pointed to the access device and asked, 'I obviously know this is an infrared sensor but do you know its frequency?'

'By any chance did you speak with my teammate Chocku?' doubted Karthik.

'You get the spare card for finding the origin of this question.'

Karthik shook his head with a smile, like it's obvious that only he can ask such a question in this office.

*

Chocku might look like monitoring the monitor but his thoughts are still about Vinoth and his business. He is trying to figure out whether Vinoth is working in a company where he is doing business or is he doing business in a company where he works? This thought has been troubling him for some time, so he wanted to vent it out to Kavita.

'Kavita, today Vinoth..' and stopped as Kavita seemed to be in deep thought .

'Kavita what are you thinking about? I haven't seen you thinking at work.'

'I am thinking about how to perform better than Vinoth.'

'Don't think about anything and do the allotted work sincerely. I am sure you will get a good rating,' advised Chocku.

'I am not concerned about ratings now man. I should sell at least one bottle of cold pressed oil more than Vinoth,' said biting the nail.

Chocku eyes fell out as if it slipped on the cold pressed oil.

'What? Do you even sell cold pressed oil in the office?'

'Yes. I came to know that today he has sold one bottle for Rs.130 to a dumb fellow.'

'How much does it actually cost then?'

'Is that you?'

'Yes, it's me.'

'You too, Chockus!' as if he backstabbed like Brutus. 'I know you are dumb but never knew to this extent. I sell it for just Rs.99. Since he has become the TL, you have bought it from him.,' said angrily. Had the stare was directed towards the oil bottle, it would have caught fire.

Karthik crossed them.

'Hey Chocku bro, sorry that the bride rejected you.'

'She might have rejected me but I am the reason for getting rejected,' told with much pride.

'I find some problem with your sense.'

'What?'

'I meant your dressing sense. Printed T-shirts would look good on you.'

'Not willing to spend much on clothes. My situation too is bad like the textile industry. Textile and clothing exports have dropped 6% during the current financial year. It has dropped from $35.9 billion dollars to..'

'STOP! Get 2 buy 1 offer is going on for T-shirts. Go to the first floor in C block, enter the ODC, take a right and in the center seat, second row to the window..'

'You too into business?'

'Yes, I know you are brilliant but you have become a Mobile Artificial Intelligence. Customized printed T-shirts. You can even check trials in the office.'

'Trial room? Here? Where?' He looked around.

'If the manager goes to eat, that becomes the trial room.'

Chocku looked in the manager's room to find an employee coming out of the room and said, 'Perfect fit bro. Will take this one.'

'Men's T Shirt, size XXL, show me the designs now,' ordered Chocku, adapting to the situation.

'Sure, I will send the designs to your phone. For pants, please contact the cloud team on the second floor. You can take the lift.'

Chocku's face went expressionless like a plain linen

T-shirt.

*

Vinoth and Jagan are in the canteen where they are surrounded by a group of guys in a table discussing about the last night match louder than the Chennai chepauk stadium. They have been in the company since its inception, so they have the leverage to work when they wish. Love is brewing between a guy from the testing team and a girl from the developer team over a machine coffee, a support fellow seated alone watching these couples and waiting for a critical priority issue *(P1 incident)* to break out between them, so that he can fix the gap.

Jagan asked Vinoth to order a coffee and vada.

'Jagan, I have left the purse in the b..'

'Know you would have left the bay in the purse. Take this cash and get me.'

'This long-term vision is what I admire so much about you.'

'Yes. We shall reduce it in the next cold pressed oil bottle.'

Vinoth left disappointed and ordered for both of them. Brought the coffee, vada, samosa and placed them on the table.

'What is this? What is the price of this vada?' Jagan agitated.

'For Rs.20, the diameter of the vada should be at least 5 cm but this is..,' Took a pen from his pocket and measured 'Not even 2.75 cm.'

Vinoth couldn't even process his weird behaviour. He tried to taste the vada, so he slid his hands to take a pinch from his vada but then took from Jagan's vada. It tasted so good that he wanted to take another pinch from his vada. He said, 'But the vada tastes..'

'Bad right?'

'Bad! Yeah, very bad. Yuk!' and kept it down.

'I Know, I Know. You know how the vada should taste. The moment it touches the taste buds, one should fall for it.'

Vinoth is unimpressed and feels silly with his description.

He continued, 'Before the spice of the vada fades away, the coffee is sipped hot, so that the spiciness of the vada and the taste of the coffee blends together to help us achieve the state of Moksha thus bringing a shiny glow in our face followed by tears rolling down the eyes.', his breath steamed out like a coffee boiler

A drop of tear from Vinoth's eyes fell into his coffee.

'And this is why I eat only Anandha Bhavan. You don't touch the food.'

Vinoth sadly kept the vada down, 'you could have at least tasted it once. Don't judge the taste by the size of the vada.'

'Don't call yourself an IT employee, if you can't figure this out. The smaller the size of the RAM, the less memory it can hold. Let's leave the place,' and got up from the seat.

Vinoth took the vada once Jagan left the table, wrapped it with paper and kept it inside his shirt pocket. As they walked towards the exit, Vinoth from behind said, 'Since we didn't eat, hope you don't reduce the amount from the cold pressed oil.'

'What form? I am already tired of filling bio-data for matrimony.'

'You need not worry about that anymore. If you fill this form, you will get cosmetic products worth Rs.5000. All you have to do is pay just Rs.500. One-time payment.'

Chocku's face grew frostbitten.

'Likewise, if you join two people under you and if those two people join another two under them, it will form a chain and as it propagates you will reap the benefits of others' work. Even if you aren't active, I can refer people to join under you. Every month you can earn with zero investment.'

Chocku heard with zero interest and wondered how to stop her.

'Wait you will understand better, if I tell you with diagrams,' and then started to draw a tree structure.

Chocku slowly moved his hand to get up and walk away from her, but she thought he was going to take the money.

'You needn't pay immediately. I know you are interested with the offer but let me finish'

Karthik stopped by, 'Rini you are early today? Has your make up kit gotten over?'

Rini is entirely into explaining the concept, 'Sshh,' she said and gestured him to leave without even looking at his face.

Chocku shook his head not to leave.

'Think she is explaining about yesterday's serial episode,' muttered Karthik and left.

'I haven't seen you much involved even while framing the architecture diagram,' cried Chocku.

'They don't give me any free products for doing it nah.'

*

Vinoth walked to his seat thinking about strange things that happened in the canteen and looked at Aysha and remembered her nodding her head 'No' when he agreed to go to have snacks with Jagan.

'Aysha, why did you nod "No" when Jagan called for a break.'

'You know, the diameter of the Dosa should be 45 cm.'

'Oh no, so you too have experienced it?' dropped himself in the chair like a bomb.

'He changed the caterer just because the dosa was not in the desired shape and I still feel guilty that I was a part of it. So far 5 caterers have changed because of him.'

'Then only if we make his wife as caterer, his expectations would be met.'

'Why his wife? Are women meant only for the kitchen? Don't stereotype.'

'No! let the manager cook for himself and we shall make his wife as manager.'

'This can be the worst solution you have ever provided.'

'I can't handle this anymore. I can handle only one person a day. That's my limit. I am already pissed off with Jagan' and as Jagan passed by, Vinoth abruptly changed his tone in a polite way.

'Hi Jagan.'

'Hey Vinoth. Have you sent the mail?'

'I have already sent the status to client Jagan.'

'No, I am referring to that canteen email. Size of the vada is our top priority. Please send an email to the admin ASAP. It should have points about the smell, touch, taste and ahm dha baa..,' blabbered.

Vinoth to Aysha, 'He has forgotten the other two.'

Jagan thought about the number of senses and got reminded about the movie sixth sense and said, 'And all the six senses.'

'If I had sense, I wouldn't have been on this team?' Vinoth told himself.

Jagan while leaving squeezed his brain hard to recollect the other senses, 'Is it wind and fire..?'

'I feel so bad for the caterer Aysha,' said Vinoth.

'You are responsible for the sin.'

'Ah while talking about sin, I got reminded about my customer Chocku'. Turned towards Kavita and spoke in a feeble voice.

'Kavita, I have sold the cold pressed oil for Rs.130 to Chocku. Please don't tell the actual price,' Sheepishly smiled.

'No way, not at all,' said Kavita with a devilish smile.

*

While all this was happening, Rini's session with Chocku was still in progress.

'That's all about multi-level marketing,' ended the session Rini. 'Aysha has joined under me and you can join under Aysha. Don't worry about finding members. If I find someone, I will add them under you.'

Chocku over a point, couldn't tolerate it, got up out of frustration and shouted, 'Is there any business that's not done in office?'

Teammates stared at him for a moment and they started discussing among themselves.

A door opened, teammates and Chocku looked to see where the noise came from.

'No one is into food delivery,' said Jagan and the teammates accepted unanimously 'Yes.'

'Okay I will start one soon,' sat down Chocku.

Vinoth reacted as if some idea had struck him to solve the canteen issue.

*

Vinoth had a parcel in his hand and he was nervous to get inside. He then gathered courage by taking a deep breath

'May I come in?' asked Vinoth.

'Yes, come in,' said Jagan.

He took the parcel out from behind like a surprise cake cutting.

'Jagan, since you expressed your dissatisfaction over the vada, the whole canteen became terrified.

'Is it?' felt as if a virtual gold medal being formed over his neck.'

'They have made a special vada exclusively for you as a token of apology. If you still don't like it, you can use your power and change the caterer.'

'How come it's going to change now? Anyways, I will try for the sake of their effort,' and took a bite by dipping it in the spicy chutney.'

Jagan experienced the exact description about vada he gave to Vinoth earlier and felt like the universe had stopped expanding for a moment. He then sipped the coffee and tears rolled down his eyes.

'This is fantastic. Recall if you have sent the mail.'

Vinoth has actually bought it from Anandha Bhavan restaurant to save the caterer.

'It tasted exactly like the Anandha Bhavan vada,' Jagan punched on the chest of Vinoth out of excitement. He felt something spongy in his pocket and he peeped to have a look. It's a paper wrapped jammed vada which Vinoth put inside his pocket.

Vinoth's face turned sweaty like an oily vada.

Jagan simply waved his hand asking him to leave with a disgusted expression.

*

CHAPTER 2 - EFFORT & CRUSH TRACKER

Rini and Karthik stepped into the canteen and Rini asked Karthik to get one cup of coffee for her too and looked around to find a place for them to sit. Karthik collected coffee from the coffee machine and turned around to see where Rini was seated. While walking towards Rini he talked to himself.

'When am I going to get rid of these coffee machines? Just for the sake it's free, I had to drink this distasteful crap.'

Placed one in front of Rini.

'Yay Coffee time,' Rini got excited.

'I know you come to the office only for break time but this expression is too much for the machine coffee.'

'But still it's a coffee,' she giggled and picked the cup with so much curiosity, 'Where is Aysha? Why hasn't she come yet?'

'Informed me that she is held up with work and would come in 5 mins. She is not Rini to leave the work unfinished.'

'Hello.'

'Oh Sorry. One should start the work to leave it unfinished. Forgot that you never start.'

'Hello' with much stress on the word 'But yeah I haven't started yet because Chocku is doing it for me.'

'Lot of tasks are pending for me. Not sure when I am going to complete it. Moreover, I am doubtful whether I will be able to complete it.'

'Hey, why do you always think about work during break? Chill.'

'You don't think about work even while you are working, but be thinking about break time. It's easy for you.'

'I am handling the work-life balance well. Okay, let's talk about something apart from work, so that you would feel relaxed.'

'Okay. Did you check the news today, there is intense tension prevailing on the India China border. The soldiers of two countries got into fist fight.'

Rini had no clue about it but nodded her head as if she understood.

'As per the article 6 of the 1996 agreement neither countries should use hazardous chemicals, guns, bombs.'

Rini interrupted to stop him. 'Ahh.'

'Ahh..Article 1 is what I was about to say too. It's mentioned that..'

'That, never go to break with Karthik?'

*

Jagan pinged over the Slack (a business communication platform) to Vinoth asking him to come to his room for an important meeting. Vinoth rushed to his room and took the seat, wondering about the purpose of the meeting.

'Vinoth, I have taken a decision after giving some serious thought. Hereafter, we need not fill the daily tracker.'

'Really?' He got off his seat out of happiness, as if Jagan had put down his paper. Daily tracker has been a burden for the whole team and it's one of the irritating tasks of Vinoth to get it done.

Jagan looked at him suspiciously and Vinoth managed by abruptly changing his tone.

'Really?' sat down casually, as if Rini had resigned. 'Then how do we track our teammates?'

'That's why, I am going to implement the hourly tracker.'

'What?' got off his seat in shock.

'What?' in a stern tone asked Jagan.

'What an idea?' abruptly enacted like he is excited about the change.

'I feel like a lot of our efforts are being wasted. I wanted to precisely know where we are wasting.'

'By speaking with you,' muttered Vinoth.

'What did you say?'

'By speaking with you I have learnt a lot about team handling. I feel so gifted.'

Jagan acknowledged like it's obvious and laughed. 'So, inform the team members and start right from today.'

'Vinoth was hesitant and sad to leave the seat as he was wondering how he is going to convey this news to his teammates and how they would take it.'

Jagan bent down to look at Vinoth's face and assumed that he had got emotional by seeing his managerial skills.

'Come on Vinoth, don't be carried away by these minor skillsets of mine. Whatever happens the work should go on.'

'Okay Jagan,' and got off his seat to leave.

'Also, regarding this meeting, enter 'Meeting with Jagan' and not 'Inspiring session with Jagan' in your hourly tracker,' laughed Jagan.

Vinoth laughed with disinterest.

'Okay the time is 10.59.'

'No Jagan, the time is 10:55.'

'Set it to 10:59 and leave the room. I have another meeting to attend at 11:00.'

'I am also part of that meeting.'

'Oh! Then go outside and come back again.'

Vinoth got furious and punched Jagan ruthlessly in his mind which even 'Quentin Tarantino' wouldn't be willing to have in his movie considering the violence.

He moved towards the door staring at Jagan.

'Take the Laptop too' told Jagan without seeing his face.

The intensity of stare increased, took the laptop, left the room and came back again.

'May I come in?' posed smile.

'Why are you late? It's already 11:01, connect to the bridge.'

'Sorry Jagan I was in another meeting.'

*

Rini is upset about Karthik talking about things that Rini is least bothered about.

'Please talk about something interesting and light hearted,' said Rini.

'As far as I know, your area of interest is the canteen and we are in that area now. What are you expecting me to talk about? Please let me know.'

'I came to know that you are hitting on someone in our office.'

'Me. No way. On what basis did you assume?'

'I have noticed your bike is often close to the same scooter in the parking lot.'

'It might be a coincidence. What if that scooter has been parked near my bike?' he stammered.

'You leave the office exactly the same time she leaves. Is that a coincidence too?'

Wondered what to say and noticed Aysha coming in, so to deviate from this context, shouted 'Hi Ayshaaa!'

Aysha walked to them asking, 'Hey why are you excited? Do you have anything to say?'

'No, I have a hot news to tell you,' said Rini.

'Hot news? Are you referring to the India China border issue?'

Karthik jumped into the conversation as he couldn't get a better opportunity to escape from the parking lot conversation. 'Exactly, a tense situation prevailing around the border areas.'

Aysha pulled the chair close to Karthik and said 'Yes. We should teach them a lesson.'

'Did you read Article 1 of 2005?' continued Karthik.

Rini got zoned off again and thought she could have gone to break with Chocku.

Chocku walked across them to get coffee. While crossing he asked 'shall we go for a break?'

Rini looked around the canteen wondering why he was asking for a break when they were already in the canteen. 'I have a server issue to resolve. Once I complete this, we shall go to the bay and have coffee,' replied in a sarcastic manner.

He pondered, how come she is working in the canteen and took time to analyse the possibility of working from the canteen and assumed, 'Oh work from canteen! You have connected your mobile to VPN to work. Great,' gestured thumbs up and left.

'I can even face the Border issue,' mumbled Rini.

*

Vinoth sent a meeting request to the whole team with the subject 'Important update' and they all gathered in the conference room in 5 minutes.

Vinoth is on one side standing worried about how to convey about the implementation of 'Hourly Tracker' to the teammates and the whole team is on the other side waiting for him to open his mouth. The teammates are wondering what could be the reason and they all start to assume.

Aysha whispered to Kavita, 'Did Jagan hurl at him?'

'He has developed thick skin for that and has no shame too. I think his wife might have joined our company.'

Chocku slowly slanted towards Karthik and signalled him to come close, 'Do you know how the clouds darken?'

'How come..?' Karthik was frustrated.

'Because..'

Stop! I was about to ask 'How come you are intelligently dumb?'

Meanwhile, Rini pondered, 'What's actually the problem between India and China?'

Vinoth sighed a deep sigh powerful enough to initiate the monsoon season.

'The corpse is up,' teased Karthik and everyone became alert as Vinoth is ready to talk now.

'So, going forward there will be no daily tracker,' announced Vinoth.

The whole team were delighted except Aysha as she felt one wouldn't work without being monitored. Vinoth, posed a sarcastic smile and sucked the decibel by dropping the next line 'But we are going to implement an hourly tracker.'

The monsoon intensified and they were hit by a hurricane.

'Can someone say that I heard it wrong?' terrified Karthik.

'You heard it right,' whined Rini.

'Can someone say he told it wrong?' Chocku brought in a new perspective to Karthik's statement.

'Vinoth!' shouted Aysha.

'You are the right person to question him. Come on Aysha,' mumbled Kavita grinding her teeth.

'Should we enter and send you every hour or enter every hour and send you the consolidated file by EOD?'

Kavita went toothless.

The daily tracker has already gone one step further with Aysha's doubt.

'What do you think will be difficult?' asked Vinoth.

'Updating every hour,' said Aysha.

'Then it's obvious, Jagan would expect you to do the same. Be prepared for it.'

'Then our only work would be to fill the hourly tracker everyday', said Kavita.

Hour 1 – Greeting each other and switching on the system.

Hour 2 - Eating snacks.

Hour 3..'

'Company will fire you,' snubbed Vinoth.

Kavita smiled sheepishly and then Chocku continued from where Kavita left, 'then Hour 4 of Vinoth will be – Hire a fresher, Hour 5..'

Vinoth took it from there to mock him, 'Hour 5 - Give KT to the fresher.'

'Hour 6 also KT, 1 hour won't be sufficient Vinoth,' Chocku raised concern.

Vinoth banged his head and Karthik stepped forward to say something.

'Now, stop extending this game to hour 7 and 8.'

Since the screen was open, his eyes glanced through the window, 'The weather looks good today. Unpredictable climate.'

'Yes Jagan,' replied Vinoth and they moved away from the bay strolling towards the exit chatting about the climate.

'Do you know how the clouds darken?' asked Vinoth.

'Oh! You know the science behind that?'

'It's a very simple concept. When the cloud is thin, the light passes through the clouds easily but when it is thick..'

They opened the exit door and strode towards the rest room as Vinoth kept explaining about science behind clouds becoming darker. As they crossed the water doctor, much involved in their conversation, Vinoth failed to notice Chocku overhearing the conversation standing aside by drinking water. To him, it sounded like hearing his recorded voice note in Vinoth's voice.

'Cloud Computing my data,' angrily muttered Chocku and placed the steel tumbler on the water doctor as if he knocked on Vinoth's head.

*

Karthik checked the time on his desktop, it's 6:30 pm. He kept on checking out at the girl in quality team who is two bays away from him. She picked her handbag and left for the day much earlier. He wanted to ensure no one is watching him while he leaves, so he checked whether Rini is noticing him but she was seen looking at her laptop and Vinoth was not in his seat. He swiftly moved away from the desk leaving his desktop turned on that blinked like a 2nd accused if caught.

He was waiting for the lift to open but to his dismay it was Vinoth inside.

'Where are you going?' he enquired.

'IIIII..,' extended as if the alphabet *I* key got stuck on the keyboard and then released to continue, 'was going to the restroom.'

'But the rest room is over there.'

'Yes, but you got me wrong. I said "I was going" past tense. After going, I came this way to..'

'To drop me in the airport,' interfered with Rini to evade him. 'Sorry for the delayed notice. My aunt is leaving to USA tonight by flight and she will be back only after years. So, I asked Karthik to drop me at the airport.'

'I thought you already got permission from him, Rini,' acted Karthik, as if he was upset. 'Sorry Vinoth, at least I should have informed you,' he posed a guilty look on his face for helping her but the real guilt lies inside Rini for trying to save him.

'Look, your action is spoiling the reputation of your colleague. I don't want this to happen again. You may depart.'

'Come, let's take off,' she hurried.

'Show the same affection towards your work too. Arrive at the office just as you go on time to send off your aunt.'

'Okay Vinoth but the flight itself is delayed by 40 minutes,' said as she ran in the steps and Karthik went behind with a hesitant smile.

After they reached the ground floor, she grabbed him by shirt collar for putting the blame on her despite trying to help him seeing his crush. He pacified her and urged that his crush would leave and her effort to save him would be wasted. Then they both go to the parking lot to see if they can create chances to speak with her. He was reluctant to go, fearing it would create a bad impression on him but Rini forced him to go and take the bike parked adjacent to her white scooter. While this was going on, a guy from behind walked past them inching towards his crush. The look in her eyes seemed like she was waiting to travel miles with him in motorcycle until she completes her life cycle and his eyes expressed as if he is willing to even exchange his number plate. Karthik and Rini realised the two lanes had already merged into one.

'You too feel the same as I do about them?' asked Karthik.

'Yes,' she nodded and lapsed into a sudden silence.

'Hey, I will overcome it someday. You don't have to worry about me.'

'Idiot. I am not worried about you. I am worried about me.'

'You? For what?' garbled Karthik and then connected the dots to figure out.

'So, were you hitting on the boyfriend of my girlfriend?' he laughed.

'Yes,' whined Rini.

'Never thought I would overcome my love failure so soon,' joked Karthik, and Rini chased him all over the parking lot. Then they both left to a food street to celebrate their love failure.

*

CHAPTER 3 – BEST OUTFIT AND SECURITY ANNA

The teammates were settled in their seats and Aysha entered the office late. The teammates looked at her in awe as she was wearing a saree. Everyone was keen to know the reason for wearing a saree to the office except Rini, as she was envious seeing her get attention. Though she was unwilling to go to her place, she looked around to see no one in their seat, so she had no option but to join them. She went and hugged her with a fake smile.

'Hey Aysha, you look so cute today.'

But Karthik and Chocku looked at each other and wondered why they act like besties. 'Cho Chweet!' they caressed each other, imitating them.

'Why in saree today? Any special occasion Aysha?' asked Karthik.

'Hey! It doesn't need to be a special occasion. I wear saree every day at home. It isn't a big deal to me. At times, I even sleep wearing it,' interfered Rini.

'Oh really? I don't have a saree, so I cover myself with a bed sheet,' replied Chocku.

'Aysha, if you tell the reason immediately, I wouldn't have to think my teammates are fools,' enraged Karthik.

'Early morning, I attended a marriage, so I came right from there. Some even said that my saree is better than the bride's but I never felt like that,' boasted Aysha.

'Me too,' said Rini.

'What do you mean?' asked Aysha.

'No. I meant; I too have got such compliments.'

'Even I have got such compliments,' said Chocku.

'The only compliment you might have got is for reserving a seat in the dining hall for your friends,' replied Karthik, and everyone laughed.

'Wait for the day when everyone says that the bridegroom is better dressed than the bride and her friends,' challenged Chocku.

'The accessories match well with your saree. You have got good dressing sense,' complimented Kavita.

'Actually, had it was contrasting, it would have been much better,' interrupted Rini and adjusted her hair near ear, trying to show them her contrasting ear ring and salwar.

Kavita ignored and kept asking Aysha about her dress and accessories.

'This too is nice Rini,' commented Chocku looking at her salwar.

'Thank you Chocku.'

'My bed sheet also has the same design.'

*

Karthik while leaving the office he noticed the night shift security replacing the day security. Had it been Karthik before getting into IT job, he wouldn't have bothered much about the life of night security workers, but since he has experienced being alone in his room, he puts himself in the shoes of the night security and imagined their difficulties.

Karthik is from Trichy and moved to Chennai for work. Though he is socially active, he preferred some privacy, so he rented a single person room. After office, he liked the 2 to 3 hours of private time. But at times, particularly during weekends loneliness would suck his soul. His mind would gradually glide into rail of negative thoughts like a corpse gliding into the electric crematorium thinking that there isn't anyone around him to lift up his mood.

Now seeing the night security worker, he was curious to know more about them, so he approached a night security. The security guard is 60 odd years old with short white hair, oil combed to his right, Vibhuti (sacred ash) on his forehead, wrinkled pale skin, mild shivering hand and stammers while speaking.

'Hi Anna. My name is Karthik.'

'Hi Sir, tell me.'

'And your name is..,' looked at his name plate on his chest that read Velumani.'

'Yes Sir.'

'Velu Anna, are you working during the night shift?'

'Yes Sir.'

'What is your work timing?'

'I work from 7 pm to 7 am.'

'Oh 12 hours of work is actually high,' surprised Karthik.

'How do you feel working during the night shift? Won't you get bored staying alone?'

The security became uncomfortable as the employees usually don't speak with the security guard apart from any office administrative issues. He was trying to figure out the purpose of asking him such a question and suspected whether he needs something out of him that requires bending the office security rules. Despite that, he answered with hesitation in his mind.

'Hmm yes sir it is boring but that's my job. The floor becomes denoised after 9 pm and we aren't allowed to lie down too, so I just sit here and be awake or walk around whenever I feel drowsy.'

'Isn't it hard to not have anyone around to speak with you for straight 12 hours?'

'Yes, but I got used to it.'

'So, weekends are the only time you get some relief. Isn't it?'

'No, we aren't given leave even on Sundays.'

'What?', shocked Karthik

'Yes Sir. We are allowed to get permission once in a month and even more than one day incurs loss of pay.'

'That sounds really harsh.'

'We have raised concerns before but they were not willing to change.'

Karthik was much worried about his mental health and that made him feel wanted to help him somehow. He thought how unfair and inhumane the system is, as they deserve off during weekends or at least on Sunday.

'How do you kill time at the office then?'

'I hear FM radio on my phone.'

'Do you have any other interest or hobby that might help you kill time?'

'Nothing specific.'

'Do you read books Anna?'

'Yes, I can read.'

'What type of books do you prefer?'

'I used to read crime novels and some weekly magazines, particularly to check the spirituality section.'

'Will you read books if I give you?'

'Okay sir,' respectfully nodded as he saw honesty in his eyes and developed complete trust in him.

*

Next day Rini arrived at the office in a saree and to gain everyone's attention, she shouted 'good morning.' It was a long greet that extended till night. Everyone looked up and replied 'good morning' formally and then got back to work. Chocku raised his hand slowly, but by looking at the monitor and said nothing. Rini was unhappy that none noticed. She got an idea and threw the water bottle near Karthik.

'Hey Karthik, can you pick up the bottle as it's difficult for me, since I am wearing saree. Karthik was surprised to see Rini.

'Hey!'

'Yes, tell me,' Rini asked curiously, expecting a compliment.

'How did the bottle fell over here?' picked up the bottle and gave it to her.

'I developed a bot that can pick and deliver bottles.'

'You couldn't develop a successful product even in your lies. Delivery failed.'

'Argh! leave it. I couldn't get why most of the auspicious times are always during early morning. It's very hard to wear this saree and go early to these functions.'

'So, you didn't go on-time to the function too?'

She gave up and said to him directly, 'Can't you see idiot? I am wearing a saree.'

"We get to wear new dress every day as we wish, but have you imagined the life of a security? They have to wear the same dress every day, including weekends. Life is unfair,' he got back to work, and Rini scratched her head.

Then to vent out her frustration, she took the bottle and went to collect water from the water doctor. While collecting, she found Chocku coming towards her. She greeted him hoping that at least Chocku would compliment.

'Hey Rini. Why in saree today?' asked Chocku while collecting the water. Rini became elated and when she was about to say, 'Wait let me guess,' stopped Chocku.

'You are going to sleep. Am I right?'

'Yes, I am on the way to the dormitory,' Rini grinded her teeth.

'But you usually sleep in the bay. Isn't it?' and the water overflowed. 'Okay see you. Sweet dreams.'

She then went straight to Kavita and asked, 'At least, did you see?'

'Yes, we all saw. So, you too saw Aysha?' excitedly asked Kavita.

While she was wondering about Kavita's excitement, Aysha entered the bay in a Bharatanatyam costume and everyone looked at her in awe.

'How did the selection go? Did you dance well?' curiously asked Kavita.

'Yes, everyone appreciated and mine will be the opening dance in Healthcare domain meet,' proudly said Aysha.

Everyone appreciated and was happy that they would get to see her dance on a big stage. Rini envied but still ran to hug her and said, 'Cho chweet'

'You look gorgeous in saree?' complimented Aysha.

Rini was touched by her words and said 'I mean it. You are really cho chweet,' hugged her again.

Jagan was in deep thinking about an issue. He then noticed Rini and called her but she came disinterested as she didn't receive compliments for wearing saree.

'You are looking great in saree today with matching bangles and earrings,' and Rini couldn't believe those words coming from Jagan as she least expected it from him, but felt delighted.

'Rini, I have a small request,' hesitated Jagan.

'You made my day Jagan. You can ask for anything.'

'One of our potential clients from South Korea is visiting our office today at 4 pm. It's an unplanned visit, so we couldn't make arrangements in prior.'

'Don't worry. I will explain the complete process.'

'No, don't commit such grave mistakes. Aysha will take care of that. I want you to welcome the client as per our custom and tradition. You are the only person I could find in a good traditional costume today.'

Rini now understood why Jagan complimented her.

'But even if the client was not visiting today, I would have complimented you anyway.'

'Okay. Thank you for the wonderful opportunity,' sarcastically said Rini.

'Hope you know the procedure to welcome as per our tradition,' doubted Jagan.

'Seriously? Do you think I don't even know to google it?'

*

Karthik while leaving the office, went to the security desk that is close to the exit door, opened his bag and took out some spirituality books he bought from a petty shop in his street and a crime novel. As Velumani was busy with work and there was another security beside him, Karthik simply placed the books near Velumani and informed him to take it. Velumani acknowledged through gestures and they both exchanged a smile.

A month later on a Friday, Karthik extended his work as the deadline of the task was by Friday EOD. The time was 9 pm and everyone had left for the day. Velumani roamed around to check if there is anyone still working, so that he can switch off the floor lights, but he found Karthik working. Velumani asked Karthik, whether he can switch off all the lights except the ones under Karthik and he accepted. After an hour, while Karthik was still working, Velumani went to his seat.

'Karthik Sir.'

'Yes Anna.'

'How much did the book cost?'

'Why Anna?'

'You have been getting me books every week. It should have cost you more. If you tell me the cost, I can give you the amount.'

'No. I didn't get you the books with that motive. I never expected any money from you Anna. It was out of my interest that I bought it for you, so that you can read when you are bored.'

'Okay Sir'

'Reading those spirituality books makes me forget my worries and gives so much peace sir.'

'Very happy to know that it makes you feel better Anna,' Karthik felt highly satisfied.

For some reason, Velumani got reminded of his son seeing Karthik, so he took a passport size image of his son from his purse and showed it to him.

'Karthik Sir, this is my son, GOWTHAM. He died in an accident a year back. He was just 33 years old with a 4 years old kid, when he left us. My grandson is staying with my daughter-in-law now. Myself and my wife are staying together, yet we feel lonely and lifeless. I ensured my son get good education and he got selected in the police department after a lot of hard work. He was a Sub-Inspector. He took very good care of us, but now he is no more,' stammered Velumani as he wiped his moist eyes.

Karthik heard it in distress, and tears lined up his eyes imagining the agony of Velumani at this age. He then got up and gave a hug to soothe him. The security then wiped his tears.

'Sorry to disturb you sir. It should be getting late for you. You carry on with your work.

'No problem anna. You can come and talk to me anytime.'

'Also, from today onwards they have allocated another security with me sir.'

'Oh really? Glad you got a companion anna.'

'Yes sir. It's that Nepali security Manish.'

'Which security anna?'

'Do you remember that day when a girl from your team wearing saree welcomed the security instead of the client by mistake,', he smiled.

'Oh yeah that security,' laughed Karthik.

Yes, Rini had welcomed the Nepali security Manish by putting the garland around his neck and placing Bindi on his forehead, who was leaving in his casual outfit after his duty, mistaking him for a South Korean Client.

*

CHAPTER 4 – BIRTHDAY AND BIRTH CHART

Karthik walked to his seat dull and Kavita's eyes traced him by biting the carrot. 'Karthik,' called Kavita and gestured to come sit in the adjacent seat. Karthik went and sat near her.

'Why are you dull? Have the dirty clothes piled up,' kidded Kavita.

'Would anyone be dull for such a silly matter?'

'Absolutely Yes! Do you know how much of my kid's clothes gets piled up in a single day?'

'Fine but that's not the problem I was thinking about.'

'Okay then tell me what's your problem.'

'Literally every day, I feel so irritated to wake up. When I go to bed at night, I pray to God for the morning to be delayed. I don't like this job, but I don't know what to pursue either. It has nothing to do with our teammates and to be honest, that's the only aspect that keeps me going, but I am not satisfied with the work.'

Kavita thought for a moment and Karthik awaited some advice from her.

'Oh, so everyone feels the same?' wondered Kavita.

'Really? I was expecting some consoling words from you?'

'Calm down. When I am in such a clueless situation, I go check astrology.'

'Astrology? Only the person who has no self-confidence would go check,' said with confidence, 'but unfortunately, I am one such person,' abruptly switched his emotion.

'I am not telling you to believe their prediction, but it may provide you a direction. It may give you some hope,' advised Kavita.

'Okay. Please refer to any astrologer you know.'

'Will send you his phone number. You can contact them directly.'

'Will he predict my future?'

'He is accurate based on my experience. He said that I would be promoted in this cycle. Based on my observation, I too feel that I would be promoted,' cheerfully said Kavita.

'Do you have the contact number of the astrologer who predicted that you won't get a promotion?'

'Yes, there is an astrologer named Jagan! Do you want to speak with him?'

'I asked for the astrologer's number and not Sani Bhagwan.'

*

Aysha while working on the SQL database, she wrote a query which involves the function MONTH (). All of a sudden, her mind deviated and began to think about special days of the current month. She strongly felt someone's birthday falls on this month, but couldn't recollect. Now without finding it she was not able to shift her focus on work. So, she asked the team.

'Guys someone's birthday falls on this month. Though I am not sure whether it's from our team, but someone I knew really well?'

'George I of Great Britain?' promptly answered Chocku.

The teammates looked at him as if they were passing intense rays through their eyes to burn him into ash. Aysha nodded her head 'No' smiling at him.

Seeing her smile he thought he was close and made another guess, 'Chandragupta Maurya?'

'Arghh! Chocku.'

'Am I that close? Is it Aurangazeb?'

'Please,' begged Aysha. It's someone I know, someone who is special to me.

'Is it Jagan,' scoffed Karthik.

'Oh wait! Exactly. Wait, how did you come up with his name,' suspiciously asked Aysha.

'Huh! I remember seeing his name in upcoming birthday mail,' sighed Karthik

'Shit. That was too close. Will insert in my database,' dispirited Chocku.

'How come it's too close?' garbled Aysha.

'Aurangazeb and Jagan both are merciless and ruthless leaders. Am I not close then?' moved close to Aysha.

'Yes, you are too close. Can you step back?' pushed Aysha and made an announcement to the team. 'Okay Team. Please share Rs.500 for Jagan's birthday celebration.'

'Show some mercy on us Aysha. Rs.500 is too much,' solicited Karthik.

'Month end Aysha. I can't afford that much. He could have been born at the beginning of some month,' muttered Kavita.

'The amount I have will be sufficient only for facial,' grieved Rini.

'Fine. At least pitch in Rs.300.'

'Okay and you too should pay Rs.300. You cannot have concession, since you are the organizer,' doubted Kavita.

'It's obvious. Why would I do that?' ridiculed Aysha.

'One person has done that before and that's why I am being cautious,' Kavita looked at Vinoth.

'Guys then the rules were different. Organisers would incur travel expenses and miscellaneous expenses. That's why I subtracted that amount from my share,' clarified Vinoth by eating the words.

'To get cake from the office canteen how come one would incur travel expenses, miscellaneous expenses, electricity expense. Cheap fellow,' mumbled Kavita.

'Is there any concession if one is going through tough times like the Astro chart is bad?' quizzed Karthik.

Aysha looked at him in confusion as if the planets were revolving around her head.

'If you don't trust, I can show you my chart tomorrow.'

'Fine. Get your Astro chart attested and upload it to the HR platform for verification. Lunatic,' enraged Aysha.

'Yes, Lunar should be the reason for everything. I think the positions of the planets Saturn and Mars with respect to the moon are causing problems to me,' muttered Karthik.

Chocku pondered like his mind was retrieving data from his brain and said, 'You guys have to be worried during August month, as there are 3 birthdays.'

'I am going to apply for vacation leave during August,' panicked Rini.

'You are already in vacation.', said Karthik

*

Next day Karthik came dull to office again with same expression and Kavita noticed it, but by biting a different vegetable

'Did you check with the astrologer? What did he say?'

'He said, 'till my last breath I will be in IT and if I try to switch, it wouldn't work for me.'

'Then go check with another astrologer.'

'Again?'

'Until I find the astrologer, who tells what I expect, I will keep checking astrology.'

'So you have referred me to the astrologer who told you what you expected him to say?'

'Absolutely. After 6 attempts, I found this astrologer.'

'So, you mean his prediction may not be correct?'

'Who cares, but it makes me feel like the angels around me are whispering that I would get promotion in the next cycle.'

'You also imply that the angels will whisper, *Karthik you will be in IT forever* in my ears?'

'Until you see the next astrologer. Yes,' smiled Kavita.

Rini breaks in, 'Seeing you work hard, I think you are going to skyrocket in your career and become my boss,' and put the hand over Karthik's shoulder.

Kavita's face lit up like she gave the right answer in the quiz wizards.

'You will be here all your life, but I will never,' shoved Rini's hand off from his shoulder.

'Okay, we shall move to another IT company dude?'

'First, I should get rid of your company.'

'Hey, why do you say that?'

'Because Rahu and Ketu are in the second house,' smirked Kavita.

'Yes, you both are my Rahu and Ketu,' angered Karthik.

Chocku walked straight to Karthik, held his face, moved left and right. Everyone is wondering, looking at his weird behavior.

'What are you looking at?' wondered Karthik.

'How come there is no white hair?'

'I never had white hair.'

'But I saw it in my dream. Your hair turned white and you were fixing the bug seated right here.'

Karthik looked at Kavita in shock.

'Now, Angel has come in the form of Chocku,' indicated Kavita.

'You might have not seen properly in your dream Chocku,' terrified Karthik.

'Oh! Then I should check my eyesight soon.'

Everyone looked confused as if they were living in a meaningless dream.

'Angel investors would be ready to invest on reading this Angel's brain activity,' mumbled Karthik to Kavita about Chocku, the angel.

'But there was one thing common in my dream and real life?' said Chocku.

"What's that?", asked Karthik.

'Even in the dream you were not able to fix the bug.'

*

Aysha waited for the Teammates to voluntarily come and give the birthday celebration amount, but there was no sign of them giving. They looked like they were ready to hold each other's hands and skip his birthday together in one long jump. So, she went directly to their place to collect the money.

'Kavita, Birthday amount please?'

'Oh, I was hoping for you to forget. Sorry, I almost forgot. Rs.300 right? Here it is,' and gave two Rs.200 notes.

'I have no change. I will give it to you later once I collect it from all.

'Ah! Then shall I give you Rs.200 now and the remaining Rs.100 later?'

'Don't worry. I won't forget, even if you *hope*,' stressed Aysha.

'Okay. I will get it from you *later soon*'. Aysha then moved on to the next person.

'If I don't get the Rs.100 back, then I am going to take at least half Kg of cake to my home,' mumbled Kavita.

'Birthday amount Karthik?'

'Oops! I left my purse..'

'I curse you that you will spend the rest of your life in this company.'

'No Wait. Hold on. Let me check my bag. That's a surprise! Couldn't believe that I had it in my lunch bag.'

'Hey Karthik, I have a doubt about the Spain project.', interfered Kavita.

'Tell me.'

'While trying to remove one of the fields from the master table, have you paid the birthday amount?' swifts her question in secrecy.

Confused about her twisted question, 'Yeah, Aysha stole it from me. And she is an angel too,' cried Karthik.

'Change is the only constant,' Kavita consoled Karthik by giving one answer for both the questions.

'Aysha, I suppose you have the change now?' smiled Kavita.

Aysha picked Rs.100 and tapped it on her hand like beating the wheat flour and moved to Chocku.

'I hope at least you give the birthday amount without any drama.'

'Sure,' took six Rs.50 notes from his purse and gave it to Aysha.

'Thank you,' smiled Aysha while moving.

'Stop,' called Chocku.

'Please give back those six Rs.50 notes, 6 notes are too much for him. I shall at least give less in the number of notes. Here it is, one Rs.500 note.'

'How do you even think like this?' laughed Aysha and gave him back the remaining Rs.200.

That's great. I gave you a single note and you have returned me one note. 1-1=0, In some way, I haven't contributed,' lifted his collar.

'To describe you in computer language, you are both 1 and 0,' laughed Aysha. 'Also had I not given you the remaining, I am pretty sure you wouldn't have asked not knowing you lost Rs.200. You are becoming predictable nowadays,' moved to the next person.

'Vinoth, Birthday amount for Jagan?'

'Take this Rs.500.'

'But we asked for Rs.300.'

'Keep the extra, but can you enter the amount given by our members in an excel sheet and share it with Jagan? We shall keep the process transparent.'

Aysha spoke nothing and gave the remaining back. 'Now, I will be transparent.'

'I like your sincerity and that is why I picked you in our team,' giggled nervously. Aysha moved to Rini's seat.

'Rini, Birthday amount?'

'My face has become tan.'

'Didn't you do your facial?'

'Usually, I do fruit facial, but to save money I did only normal facial, Keep it,' gave the money disinterested.

'You guys made me feel like collecting money for a cremation funeral. Okay, what do we gift him?' asked Aysha to the whole team.

'Get him a lens. It will be useful for him to micro-manage,' said Chocku.

'Dinner coupon,' said Karthick.

'Get a coupon from a restaurant you hate. He will ensure it is sealed. The length of the noodles should be 8 cm,' imitated Vinoth.

'How about we get him a dining set?' suggested Kavita.

'It's usual. We should gift him something that's creative and has a personal connection,' said Aysha.

'I suggested my favourite gift. Anyways, it's now easy for you guys to gift me on my birthday,' laughed Kavita.

'Shall we get him a wall clock? since he is very good in time management,' like she cracked the ENIGMA code.

'Our family is highly creative. My cousin received 60 wall clocks for his marriage,' mocked Karthik.

'It's creative, only if the clock hands rotate in anti-clockwise direction,' commented Chocku.

'Let's ask him to hang it upside down,' kidded Rini.

'Still, it would rotate clockwise,' replied Chocku and it cracked them up.

'Really?' she untied her watch and checked by rotating it upside down. Apart from Chocku, everyone else too had a look at her watch to see how it rotated as they too had thought the same.

*

The whole team except Aysha is seated inside the conference room to discuss a new project. Aysha went to buy cake for Jagan from the office canteen. Vinoth is panic stricken as he hasn't completed the effort estimation report required for the meeting. He needs to collect the effort from the teammates to provide timeline estimation but he has no sufficient data to present Jagan. He gave the responsibility to Kavita, but she couldn't get it on time and now she has buried her face inside the laptop to finish it before Jagan arrives. Rini was asked to work on SOP, but she is busy browsing the shopping sites as if she has been given a task to add at least 10 items to the wish list before Jagan gets on to the meeting.

'Do you regret working here?' asked Karthik.

'No way. I love my job,' replied Rini.

'Rini, I know you haven't completed the SOP, but do finish it by EOD today. We have already crossed the deadline. I am really worried about how I am going to pacify Jagan today.'

'I will definitely finish it by today Vinoth,' and pressed Alt + Tab shifting to the SOP document. 'I hate my job.'

'Now I feel consoled,' smirked Karthik.

'When are you sending the estimation Kavita? We are running short of time,' hurried Vinoth.

'I had to discuss with various teams Vinoth. I didn't have enough time as I was working on the Belgium project.'

'Don't say that you had no time.'

'Then what should I say?' asked Kavita, putting up an innocent face.

'Argh! My time is not good.'

'Your time is not good,' repeated Kavita, and Vinoth banged his head. Kavita buried herself into the system again.

'Karthik, have you completed the process flow?' asked Vinoth.

Meanwhile, Jagan walked inside the room smiling, by looking over the phone like a kid watching coco-melon rhymes. Vinoth has hit the panic button and his hands began to shiver seeing him come.

'Okay guys. I just need one piece of information as I have other priority work' and noticed that Aysha is missing.

'Vinoth, where is Aysha? Why isn't she here?'

'I thought not to involve her in this project, as she is already occupied with other high revenue projects.'

'No. She is our critical resource and I need her right now in the discussion,' ordered Jagan.

'I thought she is not required for this project, so I have sent her to buy a cake for your birthday Jagan.'

'Oh! then fine. Let her carry on with it. No problem,' blushed Jagan. 'What about the process flow Vinoth. Don't give answers that upsets me on my birthday.'

'The whole process flow is almost ready. The amount of work left is just equivalent to writing *Happy Birthday* on the cake.'

Jagan's eyes widened in happiness, 'Good, if it is attractive and presentable, then this project is merely the icing on the cake. What about the SOP?'

'It's ready too. I have to just attach the file and send it to you.'

'Okay. So, the work left is just equivalent to the cake delivery time,' blushed Jagan.

'When can we deliver the first release? What is the quality metric?' asked Jagan.

'Huh!' words weren't coming out, as if he gulped the empty air.

Karthik, who is adjacent to Vinoth, bent back and hid behind him to prompt, 'July 10, 95% quality.'

'JULY 10, 95% quality is the metrics,' repeated Vinoth.

'Good. That's a short span of time. Client also was expecting around that date.'

Vinoth felt relieved and breathed out a tornado.

'Who is going to coordinate this project?'

'Karthik,' answered Vinoth.

'Good. Your service is much required for the company till its last brick.'

Karthik unwillingly nodded his head as that's the last thing he would prefer.

'Angel,' whispered Kavita from the opposite seat.

Jagan looked at his phone, as it kept on vibrating. Chocku peeped at Jagan's phone and his spectacle lens zoomed in deep enough to read the processor of his phone.'

'Okay I have another important meeting to catch up on. Do submit the detailed plan by tomorrow,' and everyone felt relieved.

'I love this job,' sighed RINI

'That important meeting is about his birthday treat discussion with manager Sarita,' said Chocku.

'Hey Karthik! When did you calculate the metrics and efforts? How did you arrive at the date? Show me the work file,' surprised Vinoth.

'Based on the meeting start time and manager's birthday, on July 10, Venus eyes fall on the 11th house, so the business will be profitable.'

'What? Is this even an estimation method? Since he didn't ask anything about it, I am sparing your life. The detailed plan should accommodate the effort and quality in such a way the release date is unchanged. Go start your work now and don't believe in astrology. Only the person who fears life, goes behind astrology. You should face any problems that come in your way. If the astrologer said, *you will have a bad time* then everything around you would look negative to you and in case he said *you will lead a great life* then you would become lazy,' advised Vinoth.

'Okay Vinoth. I will be strong.'

Jagan ended his phone conversation while Vinoth came out of the hall to have a discussion regarding the delivery date.

'Vinoth, come here.'

'Yes Jagan.'

'When is the delivery date?'

'July 10. Why Jagan? Are you going to inform the client now?'

'No. I just want to check whether that day is auspicious.'

'What? Do you check Astrology?'

'Yes. Astrology is science.'

'Yes Science! Science!' nodded Vinoth.

*

Aysha informed everyone to be at 5pm for the birthday celebration in the canteen over the Slack. She then went to the canteen 15 minutes prior to the birthday celebration to collect the cake which is being kept inside the canteen fridge. All assembled in the canteen at 5 pm with not much excitement in anyone's face except Aysha and Kavita. Aysha was filled with joyous feeling, as she is inspired by his managerial qualities. Kavita hoped she would get some leftover cake, so that she could take it home.

'Is it Black Forest?' asked Jagan.

'Yes Jagan,' answered Aysha.

'Looks like 1 KG. It should be around Rs.600. So even if you had pitched in a minimum of Rs.300, it would total to..,' calculates in his mind and laughs. 'So, there should be another gift. But I am not inclined towards these gifts you see,' and looked for the gift with curiosity.

'How can one live life without any expectation?' amazed Vinoth.

'Only Vinoth can exceed the expectation of Jagan,' whispered Kavita into Aysha's ears and imitated like him by bending forward. Aysha then took the gift out from beneath of an adjacent table.

Jagan smiled to an extent that his thick moustache opened up and paved the way for his glittering teeth to showcase. He unwrapped the gift with excitement in his eyes.

'Oh it's a wall clock. Ha ha that's a timely gift,' and the teammates laugh hesitantly at his joke.

'Okay may I cut the cake now. I have important work to complete.'

'I too have an important task to pack it,' drooled over the cake Kavita.

'You may all sing now,' ordered Jagan, and the teammates started to sing, 'Happy birthday to you..'

Jagan skimmed through each one of them to check whether all are singing and found out Chocku was keeping his mouth mum. Chocku noticed him checking his lips and he started singing.

Jagan then took a piece of cake and gave it to Aysha. 'For making all the arrangements and singing beautifully.'

Teammates were surprised and looked at Vinoth, but he enacted like enjoying the moment as if the tears were flowing straight inside his heart.

'Somebody cut and distribute the cake please.'

'I will,' chipped in Kavita and cut the cake into small pieces and started distributing.

'Treat! Treat!' shouted Karthik, hiding behind Vinoth.

'Ha ha sure. I will take you all to a barbeque, but only on my birthday and not today,' revealed Jagan.

Teammates were puzzled.

'Isn't today your birthday?' asked Aysha.

'Yes. My certificate birthday. I haven't told anyone for years. If you can make my certificate birthday so special, I am pretty sure to have a blast on my original birthday,' laughed Jagan. 'I just wanted to create some fun moments in our team as we have been having a hectic schedule in recent months.'

All have no option but to laugh hesitantly. He then received a call and picked the phone. While attending the call he excused by saying, 'Birthday wishes pouring. I will be right back,' he informed them and walked aside.

'At least I should compensate for the amount I paid,' thought Kavita and opened a tiffin box to fill the box with cake.

'Let's not waste the cake. I will take it home.'

'Please preserve this cake. Let's cut the same cake on his original birthday,' annoyed Rini

'Karthik, I have a serious doubt. So, you must have calculated the delivery date by considering the Astro chart of his duplicate birthday and not his original birthday then?' feared Vinoth.

'I know you are testing me whether I am still into astrology. I have stopped thinking about it after your advice,' and left to grab a piece of cake from Kavita.

'Astrology is science da.', his voice broke

Meanwhile, Kavita filled two tiffen boxes with cake and announced, 'I hereby donate one of the cake boxes to the most affected victim of this drama Ms. Aysha,' laughed Kavita.

Jagan came back after the call, 'Okay guys. Thanks for the wishes and celebration. Enjoy the cake. I have another cake cutting to catch up on the 3rd floor,' and hurried towards the lift.

'Jagan, when is your actual birthday?'

'It falls on August 30th,' shouted Jagan as he rushed

The shock waves of all the team members were in synchrony with each other, as one more birthday gets added to the month of August.

*

CHAPTER 5 - WATER BOTTLE AND BOTTLENECK SITUATION

Vinoth while allocating work for each member, he stopped for a moment and felt pity about Karthik as he is going to be assigned the toughest task ever. He pinged Karthik to come to his place over the Slack.

'Karthik, I am assigning an important task for you today.'

'I don't remember you assigning me an unimportant task in the past. Everything is important according to you.'

'Okay then this is the most important of all the tasks I have given you. I have collected the monthly tasks update from all the members except Chocku. So, your task is to get his monthly report.'

'That's it? Get tasks updated for the month from Chocku? Nothing technical? It's a matter of minutes,' snubbed Karthik as if Vinoth is overrating a terrible movie.

'Minutes collectively form hours and hours collectively form a day, so you take a day's time.'

'Oh! come on. He is going to provide me with the details if I conduct a one on one meeting with him. As simple as that.'

'One on one? Sounds like a wrestling fight to me. I would be the happiest person if you knock him out in the first round. Carry on. Round 1, fight.'

'I wish you would give me this sort of work every day, so that I will finish it in an hour and chill for the rest of the day.'

'If you complete this task successfully, then you can take this responsibility going forward.'

'Pchh! You better be ready with another unimportant task for me in an hour.'

*

It's morning 10 am and Kavita entered the office walking towards the ODC with a flat face as if the nature is pushing her forward with no little effort from her and Jagan came opposite wishing her 'Good Morning Kavita' authoritatively, but she turned her eye to his direction like a doll with no life in it and doesn't wish him back as she was grieving about something. Once Kavita reached her seat, Aysha sensed that she is abnormal today.

'Good morning, Kavita! How was your weekend?'

She simply waved her hand and made gestures conveying that she won't talk today.

'You won't speak? Why?' asked Aysha, and Kavita conveyed her through gestures that she has taken vow of silence and won't reveal the reason as it might spoil the cause and nodded her head with a frown face.

'Hi Kavita,' greeted Rini.

'Kavita is in a vow of silence today. She has wished for something personal I suppose,' explained Aysha.

'Oh okay. You usually tell motivational quotes every day and that would give me energy for the rest of the day. It's been a long time, so I thought I shall hear from you today.'

'Kavita made gestures to tell her a motivational quote and Aysha translated, 'Push yourself because no one is going to do it for you!' and the tears kept flowing while she was conveying.

'Rini and Aysha realised that she is in deep trouble and both consoled her that things will be alright soon.

'Kavita, Is the Belgium process flow chart done? We have to present it to Jagan today,' enquired Vinoth.

Kavita gestured again to tell him the status, but Vinoth misunderstood, 'Hey, I didn't come for snacks this time.'

'No, she is in silence fasting for some personal reason,' translated Aysha.

'What nonsense is this? She has to make an important presentation today to Jagan?'

Kavita slowly turned her head towards Aysha. 'Me? No, I already have a load of work to do.'

'I have already informed Jagan that you are going to present. Push yourself because no one else is going to do it for you,' said Vinoth.

'Did you hear the quote from us?'

'Oh, I didn't know it came from here,' blinked Vinoth 'but that quote came straight from my heart.'

Kavita looked helpless and Aysha understood that she was in deep trouble and decided to help her.

'No issues Vinoth. I will do the presentation on behalf of her.'

Kavita looked at Vinoth in a pleasing manner.

'But..,' Vinoth's eyes were searching for something at her desk.

Kavita opened the snacks box. 'Butter biscuit!' exclaimed Vinoth and picked one from the snacks box. 'Kavita, please give KT to Aysha in any mode of communication. Aysha this a good opportunity, so make use of it,' remarked Vinoth and left to his seat with the snack box.

Kavita conveyed that she is thankful to her.

'I see this as an opportunity to help you. I would be happy if things happen as you wish,' expressed Aysha.

Karthik scheduled a meeting from 10.30 am to 11.30 am and sent an invite to Chocku. His inbox received an invite rejected mail in a blink of an eye. Wondered the reason for rejecting and met him in person.

'Chocku, I need an update on all your tasks for the month.'

Chocku picked up the water bottle to drink and Karthik witnessed the water go swirling into his mouth.

'What were you asking? Come again.'

'I need an update on all your tasks for the month, shall we have a meeting now? I already sent you a meeting invite, but you rejected it abruptly.'

'Okay. I might have done it due to work pressure.'

'Oh fine. Then I will send you now, please accept.'

'No, I will reject it again.'

'But why?'

'Because I am under work pressure. Can you hold it for a moment?' froze Chocku as if he had stepped on a landmine, but there was motion only in his eyes which were rolling to observe the reactions going on inside his body. 'My bladder has reached its limit. Body metabolism. Move,' and rushed to the restroom.

Karthik went back to his seat and kept an eye on Chocku's seat waiting for him to come back. Once he came back, he again went to Chocku.

'Chocku, please give your update.'

'Update? Research says, our body should maintain 60% of water content.'

'All my water content is going out in tears. Please provide an update.'

'Then you may require this,' handed over the water bottle to him and rushed to the restroom again.

Karthik realised it's all because of the water. So, he tried to drink all the water in one gulp spilling all over his shirt, but succeeded in emptying the bottle. 'Now let me see how his bladder gets filled again,' mumbled Karthik. As every second counts, Karthik asked the moment he sat on his chair 'Did you complete the Technical SOP of ITALY project?'

'Body metabolism you see,' and got up again.

'But you never drank water this time?'

'I drank in the water doctor while I came out of the rest room.'

Now Karthik sensed the water getting filtered and dripping into his urinary bladder. This time he also rushed to the restroom trailing Chocku.

Karthik took the urinal adjacent to where Chocku was standing. Tried to open his mouth and ask for an update, but felt that germs could go inside. He then gathered courage to ask him.

'Chocku, what is the update for the B&B Italy project technical SOP?'

The sound of urine falling went mute. He slowly turned and stared at Karthik. 'Is this the right place to ask such details? You are increasing my blood pressure despite not adding salt in food,' pulled up the zip angrily and got back to work.

'I am not going to complete this task by today. At least let me finish the task of emptying my bladder,' Karthik pumped out all his pressure by letting out the salty liquid, hoping it will decrease his blood pressure.

*

Kavita pondered that she could have taken off today as this has become a burden for the team, especially for Aysha. She wished for the day to run fast, so that her vow of silence doesn't lead to any other issue.

'Kavita, Jagan wants to speak with you,' said Vinoth. Kavita is worried as to how she is going to tackle Jagan without talking and became nervous.

'Oh My God! Why is he calling me,' translated Aysha.

'Reading the mind voice is too much,' said Vinoth.

'I give my best to any task I am assigned to do.'

'Oh really! Now go with her and give your best to Jagan too.'

'No. Why should I go?'

Kavita looked at Aysha in a pleasing manner and Aysha accepted to come with her to meet Jagan.

Kavita walked front and Aysha behind to his room. Kavita opened the door and had eye contact with Jagan for a few seconds. Jagan waited for Kavita to talk as he was upset with her for not responding to him in the morning.

'May I come in?'

Jagan wondered from where the voice came as Kavita lips had no movement but only made gestures. Then, Aysha entered from behind Kavita.

'Come in Aysha, but you may go out. I never asked you to come.'

The person, whom I asked to come, hasn't asked me permission to get in and doesn't have the manners to respond when one greets. Kavita turned towards Aysha and gestured her to respond.

'He is asking, please respond to him,' translated Aysha.

Kavita looked frustrated at Aysha.

'Oops! Sorry, I actually came here as a translator for her. She asked me to talk about something, but I translated that too as I was nervous. She has taken a vow of silence today due to some personal reason.'

'What?' shouted Jagan. 'How can one work without talking? How will you do the presentation today then?'

'I will present on behalf of her.'

'Why not you take the vow of silence on behalf of her?' directed his anger towards Aysha. 'And you Kavita, in that case, don't you have the brain to take off today?'

Kavita responded to Jagan through gestures, but this time Aysha stared at Kavita for the crazy answer she was trying to give.

'You don't have enough leave? Seriously, is that even a reason and you want me to tell this to him?' angrily whispered Aysha in her ears. To save her, she didn't translate this time but said, 'This presentation was the reason,' and Kavita was relieved as she gave a better reason.

'Now I badly want to know the reason for your silence. Do tell me once that happens as per your wish,' said Jagan and gestured like Kavita, asking both of them to leave.

'Thank you, Jagan,' said Aysha.

'Jagan looked at Kavita, as her 'Thank you' is pending. So, Kavita bent to Jagan and Aysha translated 'Thank you' on behalf of Kavita and Jagan responded by bending like she did.

*

Karthik was staring at his monitor hopelessly, as he was unable to get an update from Chocku.

'Are you chilling out?' sarcastically asked Vinoth.

'If you could give me two days?'

'Hmmm, how many times did he go?'

'Please help me,' blubbered Karthik.

'Okay. Don't worry. I will help you get an update from him. I will help you,' consoled by tapping on his shoulder.

'You are the lead of this team. Won't he send you in a jiffy, if you ask him to provide an update?'

'Karthik, every individual is unique. It's more important to learn how to handle people than doing the technical tasks assigned to us. Now, talk to him as I say, you can get the update from him.'

'Okay Vinoth.'

'Now the first step is, we both should go to Urinal.'

They both found Chocku in the urinal as expected and stood adjacent to him. Vinoth to the left side and Karthik to the right side of Chocku.

'Karthik did you check the news today? There are millions of galaxies identified through the Hubble telescope,' asked Vinoth.

'Really?' replied Karthik.

'Give correct information Vinoth,' interrupted Chocku. 'There are precisely 200 billion galaxies and we have a better picture in the James Webb telescope.'

'Wow. We are finding it difficult to even identify a bug in the ABN Belgium project.'

'Ah! Not a big deal. I have found the bug and fixed it myself. Will push to production today.'

Vinoth signaled Karthik to make a note of the update he just gave.

'Did you check the Top 10 destinations of the world list released by a tourism survey.'

'London, Paris, Crete, Bali, Rome, Phuket, Sicily, Majorca, Barcelona, Istanbul,' listed Chocku.

'Where is Sicily?' asked Vinoth.

'Italy,' promptly replied Chocku.

'We will never go to Italy in this birth for sure. At least we get to work in an Italy project', said Vinoth and waited. All the energy in both their bodies accumulated in the ear to the side of Chocku hoping they would get an update

'Yes, but their tool isn't as impressive as their country. I am working on the root cause analysis of recurring issues and it may take a week time.'

'Then?' Vinoth was thinking about which project to ask next.

'Then, a Swedish scientist discovered that an artificial ozone layer can be formed. Very interesting read. And regarding the Sweden project, I have included a new functionality in the tool to automatically generate report from their end,' zipped his pant and left as the bladder was emptied for the nth time.

'Sweden update is a bonus for us. If you follow this for 3 more times, you can get all the updates for the month,' suggested Vinoth to Karthik.

'But how do I act like peeing often for a long time.'

Another person came in between them and they looked to find it's Jagan.

'Did you receive the updates from Chocku,' asked Jagan as if he was spying on the world's most dangerous criminal.

'In progress. Will be completed by today,' said Vinoth.

'Good. Disperse,' Jagan left in secrecy.

*

All the team members are in the conference hall to attend Aysha's presentation which was supposed to be presented by Kavita. Aysha began the presentation.

'Our tool should pull the data from the 6 sources mentioned by the client..'

Kavita received a call and she picked it up without a second thought. Aysha stopped her presentation as she felt interfered. Vinoth and Jagan got irritated by the behaviour of Kavita, but she kept talking over the phone hesitantly, gesturing to excuse her for the call.

'Really?' spoke Kavita. The team is surprised as she has broken her vow of silence.

'Yayyyy! My son has poooooped,' screamed Kavita.

The teammates made a disgusting face.

'Shit! I have never had such a smelly day in my life,' nauseated Karthik.

'Shit,' Rini took perfume from her handbag and sprayed it on her and the surroundings.

'He was constipated for 4 days. We were so afraid,' revealed Kavita.

'Now I understand the actual meaning for your quote: *Push yourself because no else is going to do it for you,*' recollected Rini.

'Jagan, Kavita's son has shit out after 4 tough days. This is the reason for her silent fasting. I have completed my responsibility as assigned,' reported Aysha.

'That's a happy news! That's a happy news! You can go to your house now if needed. I can feel your pain,' emoted Jagan as he too had gone through it with his kid.

'Where is Chocku?' asked Vinoth.

'He should have gone to pee,' replied Karthik.

'If one has a child that goes to the restroom like Chocku, then there is no need for silence fasting,' kidded Vinoth.

'You two go and get the update from him,' urged Jagan. Vinoth and Karthik rushed out to get the update.

*

CHAPTER 6 – BAY DECORATION AND CRITICAL PRIORITY ISSUE

It's Monday morning and Rini was in deep thought at her desk thinking about the incident that happened two days back in her PG hostel. The rule of PG is to not use an induction stove, iron box or any other electrical equipment but her roommate Vaishnavi was using an iron box. Rini usually gives her clothes to an ironing shop near her PG but occasionally uses the iron box in case of emergency. On Friday, her roommate had kept the iron box inside her cupboard after using it. Rini returned to the PG before Vaishnavi, found the room was in a mess as if someone had searched their room for diamonds. Both of their cupboards and suitcase were open. She then checked if anything was lost and gladly all her things were safe. When she reported it to the warden, she came to know that it was the warden who had unlocked their room to search for electrical equipment. The warden had a set of keys with her for cleaning purposes. Rini found the iron box in the warden's room. She was pissed off and got into a verbal fight with the warden for opening her suitcase and cupboard. Her roommate who came later though was frustrated didn't vent out her anger like Rini did as the mistake was hers too. Rini then decided to vacate the PG immediately as her ego didn't allow her to stay and she also felt being controlled. She then moved to an independent small 1 BHK house with the help of her Dad and Karthik where she was staying alone. Since she always wanted people to be around it was difficult for her to be alone and hated going back to her room. While all this was going on in her mind, a mail popped up snapping her mind to present.

'Hey guys. Did you check the mail?' excitedly asked Rini.

'Since you are looking at it after a long time, the mail box looks exciting to you. We check our mails daily,' teased Karthik.

'Idiot. I meant the HR mail. Check them.'

'You must be the only person to check HR's mail.'

'They have sent the list of talent showcase events for Diwali.'

'Talent? Then how come it's related to you?'

'I am going to register my name in Badminton and win it.'

'This is not a lucky draw. You have to play.'

'What are all the events they are conducting this time?' asked Vinoth, and everyone skimmed through the mail.

'Variety talent contest, Carrom contest, Badminton contest..'

'UAT test', interrupted Chocku.'

All look at Chocku like *can't throwing tomatoes on Chocku be a contest?*

'I am working guys,' clarified Chocku.

'Am I here to have some fun?' remarked Rini.

'Looking your task status, it seems so.'

'I have no time to fight with you. I have a lot of work to do'.

She got up and went near Karthik.

'So, disturbing me is your work. What do you want? Tell me.'

'We have 2 weeks of time for the competition. Why not buy bats, shoes and practice in a shuttle court for the event?'

'Do you want to buy it on Diwali and burn it on Bhogi? *(On the occasion of Bhogi, people discard their old and useless household items, wood, and clothes among others)*

'Pchh!' turned and addressed the whole team. 'Hey someone from our team, please register your names in events. Aysha, aren't you registering for dance?

'No, since I have back pain, the doctor has advised me not to dance Bharatanatyam.'

'What about you Chocku?'

'I will get back pain if I dance, so I am not participating.', said Chocku, and everyone were in splits.

'Kavita, what about you? Give your name to any of the events.'

'Give me leave on that day. I will get rest at least for a day'. As Rini came close to her, she whispered, 'Make Vinoth join in any of the events, so that we all will be free on that day.'

'What is his skill?' puzzled Rini.

'He knows to play musical instruments.'

'You mean this,' Rini gestured like playing JALRA *(It is a percussion instrument. It has two cup shaped cymbals connected by a cord passed through centers. They are played in the background constantly, so as to produce a ringing sound. The instrumentalist is comically associated to person who nods the head to everything one says)*

They laughed in a controlled manner as if the speed of the burning stove was reduced from Max to Sim level.

'Hey guys. Please don't tell me we are not giving names for Bay decoration. At least we shall participate together in an event,' pleaded Rini.

'No. In case there is an escalation to our dismay, then he would say it's because of us blowing balloons. He will blow things out of proportion. I have experienced it once,' feared Vinoth.

Jagan overheard him and felt bad about it. He then came to the bay.

'Hey guys did you check the Diwali mail?' enquired Jagan.

We haven't registered for any events, Jagan. Our productivity will go down,' assured Vinoth.

'Let's manage it man. I will register our team's name in Bay decoration. We are winning this time. Okay?'

'Yes Jagan' said the team and all became happy as they didn't expect Jagan to show involvement.

'Then shall I give my name for playing Music Instrument?'

'Of course, you can. Why do you have to ask me? Go ahead. You are well known for playing instruments. I enjoy hearing you play.'

Rini and Kavita look at each other and chuckle, relating it to Jalra. And then they both split abruptly moving away from the spot even before Vinoth could notice them laughing.

By noon, Rini went to Karthik's desk.

'So, will you win?' asked Rini.

'Why only me? We all are going to be part of it. We will win.'

'I am talking about your solo variety show.'

'Me? But I never gave my name,' confused Karthik and noticed Rini chuckling non-stop to realise.

'Hey, did you register my name?' shocked Karthik.

'You are often worried about this IT work. Why not try something in which you are good at. I find you are good at entertaining people, so why not give it a shot. If you keep pushing your days by wailing, nothing is going to change. Who knows, this can be a first step towards change. Even if it's not going to change anything, it would at least ease yourself from this work pressure.'

'But what will I perform? I haven't been on stage before. In fact, I have only mocked the performers from the last row.'

'Then that's your karma. Better face it,' laughed Rini. 'See, you make the people around you happy by cracking jokes and pulling their legs. Do that on stage. This can lead you to something. It can be of any form. RJ, VJ, acting and anything related to media. I am sure you will figure out something that drives you.'

'Doing it on stage is different. I don't want to face any insults on-stage.'

'Not more than the insults I have faced.'

'How can one tell it with much pride? How should I acquire this talent?'

'IT interpersonal skills. Idiot, Are you performing or not?'

'When the right time comes, I will try.'

'There is nothing called the right time. In each stage of life, you will have a responsibility. And, I am not telling you to quit the job. Just try out your skill in the office and see where it takes you. If not, find the driving force to like the IT job.'

'Okay, I will try.'

'Good.'

'I have never seen you talk about something serious like this before. Did you watch any motivational videos?'

'If you motivate me to watch, maybe I will consider it.'

*

Aysha, Rini and Kavita discussed the decoration and listed out the items required. Aysha provided the list to Karthik and asked him to buy those items next morning without fail. Karthik purchased at night and brought it the next morning. Aysha cross checked the items with the checklist.

'Balloons?' asked Aysha.

'Yes,' replied Karthik.

'Serial lights?'

'Yes.'

'Colour papers?'

'Yes.'

'DB issue?' interrupted Vinoth.

Slowly turned towards him 'No,' worried Karthik. Aysha gave an intense look as if she was going to hang him with the decoration.

'Jagan himself is not much concerned today, why are you bothered?' questioned Aysha.

'If this DB issue is resolved, he is free for the whole day.'

'Okay fine. You are free right?'

'No, I want to check whether he is working, by keeping my eyes open.'

'First keep your eyes open, walk with your legs to the store and get me 5 double sided tapes.'

Karthik rushed to his place and started working on the issue. In a hurry, instead of deleting the table in the UAT environment (mock environment) he deleted the master table in the production environment by mistake. He then checked twice whether he had really deleted the Production table but unfortunately, yes .It took him few minutes to realise the blunder. He started to sweat and shiver. His brain couldn't process the next step. He turned towards Kavita and somehow pulled out a few words from his gut.

'Kavita, I have deleted the master table in production by mistake,' trembled Karthik.

'Oh my God! So, no rest today too?' worried Kavita and she noticed Karthik was shaken.

'Okay wait. Let's resolve it. Don't worry,' pacified Kavita.

She took the seat and started working. Karthik could see thousands of logics running in the mind of Kavita, until she said, 'Chocku, can you please come here?'

Karthik lost the hope of this resolving any time soon.

'We will discuss and resolve it. Patience is important at this point of time,' Kavita calmed the nerves.

Aysha came to Karthik's seat to ask about how long would it take to complete the work, so that she can get help from him for decoration. In the meanwhile, Chocku also had come as Kavita called him.

'Yes Kavita. Why did you call me?' asked Chocku.

'Karthik has deleted the master table in production by mistake.'

'Oh No,' shocked Aysha.

'Thanks for the update,' Chocku left the place.

'Hey Chocku!' shouted Aysha and Kavita.

'She has called you for help. Not to update you,' said Aysha.

'Please see if you can resolve it, Chocku,' requested Kavita.

'Please be clear when you convey information. Move,' said Chocku and took the seat from Kavita.

'You go and inform Vinoth. This has to be updated to him immediately,' said Kavita.

'Vinoth has gone to get double sided tape.'

'Can someone get me my water bottle?' Chocku raised his hands.

'Uff! Can someone call and inform Vinoth to buy a bedpan too?' because Karthik knew he would go to the restroom often.

Jagan came to the bay to check the progress of bay decoration. Vinoth is also back from purchase.

'How is the bay decoration going? Feel free to ask me for any support.'

'Jagannn!' Karthik stretched his name as if it contained 289 characters. 'Still 100 more balloons to blow Jagan,' told Vinoth as he isn't aware of the master table deletion issue.

Others were irritated with his reply.

'You want me to blow balloons. It's a simple task. Let me do it,' Jagan extended his hands for balloons.

'No Jagan. We actually have a serious issue,' hesitated Kavita.

'You want me to put out the serial lights? I can do that too,' and started to blew one of the balloons.

'No Jagan. Karthik deleted the master table in production by mistake.'

The balloon flew away from his mouth and became speechless. His neck moved like a lighthouse towards Vinoth, 'Aren't you aware of what's happening in the team?'

'I was absent on that day. Sorry, I went out to purchase Jagan.'

'Okay leave it aside. Support him and recover the data as soon as possible. I myself will mail the client. Don't worry. Just focus on the work. And I will come and blow the balloons. That's my responsibility.'

Teammates felt relieved with the way he handled the situation.

'So, the bay decoration is on,' said Rini.

'No worries. These sorts of issues happen at times. It's quite common,' Vinoth patted on Karthik's shoulder.

'Can I be of any help to you guys?' asked Rini.

'Yes,' Aysha handed over the colour papers and evaded her from that area.

Chocku is still trying his best to resolve the issue and Karthik is seated behind Chocku biting his nails. Rini then called Karthik and gestured to come.

'Did you practise well?' enquired Rini.

'Do you have any idea about what's going on here? The moment I deleted the table, I deleted the performance from my mind too.'

'So what? If you step back from such problems, then you will be afraid for life long.'

'But I feel bad, as I am the reason for this mishap,' frowned Karthik.

'Hey! Team will take care of this issue. This is a very insignificant issue in your life. Performing despite all these problems will only make you stronger. You hold on for a minute,' Rini walked to Vinoth.

'Vinoth, Karthik has registered his name in Variety talent.'

Vinoth looked at Karthik, but he put his head down in shame.

'He will be back in 30 mins.'

'Back in 30 mins?'

'Yes Vinoth.'

'You should be back in 30 minutes with prize winner. Only that can compensate for the trouble you created. Chocku will take care of this. You can go participate.'

Chocku turned his head and said, 'Simple Issue', to Karthik to pacify him and abruptly switched to the monitor in panic.

'Go. Do well,' motivated Rini.

'Yes, I am going,' Karthik gets pumped up.

'Showcase your talent.'

'I am going to show.'

'Channelize all your energy, stress and anger in your performance.'

'Yesss!' shouted aggressively and then stopped abruptly.

'But can you come with me? I am nervous,' begged Karthik.

*

Karthik got on the stage and joked about the cafeteria, admin, HR, manager, freshers, catering service etc and they were in splits. Once his performance was over there was a huge applause and he came down with great satisfaction. Rini felt so happy seeing the response.

'You did great dude,' congratulated Rini with a wide smile.

'The next performance is by Rini,' announced HR.

'Oh, looks like there is someone else too with the name 'Rini,' said Rini innocently.

The employees on the floor looked at her.

'Why is everyone looking at me? No, it's not me,' mumbled Rini.

HR called out Rini from production support.

'Sorry Rini,' apologised Karthik.

'I was expecting thanks from you, why are you saying sorry?' wondered Rini.

'I registered your name to avenge, but I completely forgot to tell you.'

'What the heck?'

'Please do something and manage. Go now,' clapped Karthik and pushed her forward.

She went onto the stage crawling like a snail walking on a treadmill.

'Once I did stand-up comedy in a stand up meeting..,' continued Rini.

'Stop,' said HR.

'Didn't you register your name for Singing?'

'Singing? Yes, singing,' smiled sheepishly. 'I thought to warm up the audience and then sing.'

'No, you can start singing.'

Once Rini started to sing, her sound waves disrupted the wavelength in the room and it got back to normalcy only after she forgot the lyrics. She then simply hummed the tune and vanished from the hall once she got down.

*

The whole team is now ready to make a presentation about their bay decoration to the chief guest. The team has dressed themselves based on the Diwali theme. Jagan as Ravana, Vinoth as Ram, Aysha as Seetha, Karthik as Laxman, Chocku as Hanuman, Kavita and Rini as people of Ayodhya.

'Who is the Chief guest Jagan?' asked Vinoth.

'He is an annoying fellow. He once said that I play a double game and I am two faced. Since then, we have never been on good terms. Moreover, he would tell some pathetic jokes and laugh at himself.'

'You are going to surprise us. Am I right?' doubted Vinoth with a smile.

'All the ten heads stared at Vinoth. Do you think all my ten heads are dumb? Why do I have to dress up like this, If I am the guest? Don't you know that the chief guest would be someone who is not related to our domain?'

'Chief guest entered and the teammates were alerted by his presence. His name is Praveen Kumar alias PK. Carries a suspicious look on his face, wears a spectacle with no reflection, his head looks like a spectacle with reflection. There is no boundary between his forehead and head. The few hairs on both the sides of the head hangs like the price tag in the spectacle. Has a thick beard that seems like his head would have looked ideal had it was tilted upside down. Some grey hairs on beard looks like he is in prior to the last stage of IT stress. Symptoms of first stage are grey hair, second stage hair fall, third stage grey hair on beard and last stage beard fall. Fat and chubby, the belly is curved enough for a kid to slide and play. He wore a yellow shirt and a white dhoti lined with golden colour on that day.

Rini welcomed Praveen Kumar by taking *Aarathi* (Holy fire on a plate) and he blew off the fire.

'Fire will trigger the water sprinklers. I can't bear the cold,' commented PK.

'Deepavali' means Deepam and..,' Aysha came forward to explain about their theme.

'Stop! Oli, it is a festival of lights. Diwali symbolises the spiritual victory of light over darkness, good over evil, and knowledge over ignorance. From the same Wikipedia which you have mugged up. I am hearing this for the 5th time today,' commented PK.

Aysha spontaneously found a way to handle it.

'You got us wrong PK. I was about to tell you that you must have already known about it. Have you ever heard the story of Ramayana from the perspective of his wife Sita?'

'No,' PK asked curiously.

'Let me tell you now' and turned back to whisper in the ears of Kavita and Rini. They both nodded their heads as if she was giving some instruction.

'I am Sita, the beautiful wife of Rama,' continued Aysha.

'I don't like such self-appraisal behaviour,' remarked PK adjusting his spectacle.

'PK, she has always been known for her beauty,' said Aysha with pride.

'Oh really! Your self-appraisal is accepted by the manager. You can get into the character. Tell me ma, what happened to you?'

Aysha angrily turned towards Jagan and pointed at him. 'This demon Ravana abducted me to Lanka in the disguise of a sage to marry me.'

'Harassment. You have breached the code of conduct, two-faced fellow,' said PK in a stern voice.

'No ten faced,' replied Jagan and then suspected whether he was referring to his nature.

'You could have been a bit careless, sorry caremore. Poor security system. Didn't you have a firewall to protect?'

'I did draw a mantra line to protect her,' said Karthik, who is playing the role of Laxman.

'You should have placed something physical. Like a wall, table or something.'

Karthik felt bad and punched on the table, as he was reminded about his table deletion.

'This is my husband Lord Rama,' pointed at Vinoth.

'Vinoth, who was standing behind her, softly said, 'My wife is so possessive. If my wife come to know about this, she will not spare my life'

'Rama?' PK pointed at Vinoth and queried, as he was not convinced with his physique. 'He is Rama?' stressed on his dissatisfaction again.

Vinoth stood stiff and pumped up his chest to appear manly.

'Aiyo Rama!' PK gestured like praying to God to tolerate this costume.

'Did you call me?' Vinoth came forward.

'What's the use of coming now? You didn't go on time when Ravana abducted her.'

'Then after 11 months, Lord Ram with the help of Laxman,' Aysha pointed at Karthik, 'and his devotee Hanuman,' pointed at Chocku.

Chocku responded by simply raising his hand and turned back to work on the critical issue.

'They fought with Ravana and brought me back,' continued Aysha.

Praveen Kumar is upset looking at Chocku as he wasn't attentive and felt disrespectful.

"Looks like Hanuman is busy flying somewhere else. Hmmm,' PK expressed his concern.

'I don't bow to anyone except Raman and Laxman,' replied Chocku by typing on the keyboard.

'And when we came back to Ayodhya, people lit lamps and celebrated our arrival,' Aysha snapped her fingers.

The serial lights in the bay lit up as she signalled.

Praveen Kumar's eyebrow raised as if his mind bulb was switched on and looked around in awe. 'But where are the people?' queried PK.

'Here sir,' shouted Kavita and Rini. Two heads peeped out under the desks, where the plug point was located. One head from each side of the bay. Aysha had given them responsibility to switch on the decoration lights.

'I loved your presentation ma. But the only thing that disturbs my mind is,' and looked at Hanuman working without bothering about him.

'Hanuman always serves Rama and the people, that's why he is working hard for us,' said Kavita.

Praveen Kumar walked to his seat and looked at what he is working on.

'The syntax is wrong. Close this bracket, use the right join and include this function. Execute,' PK hit the Ctrl + E.

'Yay! The data has recovered!' cheered Chocku. 'You are the real Hanuman sir,' embraced PK.

The whole team felt relieved and thanked PK for resolving the issue.

'Thank you so much PK,' said Vinoth.

'I never announced you guys as the winner.'

"We are just reel God Sir, but you are our real God. Particularly, for me, you are my native village God,' Karthik shook with his two hands.

'You have made our day,' Jagan wished PK.

'But you have spoiled years of happiness Ravana. You are the reason for all the mishaps.'

'No don't trust their story. This is just the front end of the story. You should also hear the back end from my perspective too. I have been projected as an evil power. There are many hidden facts.'

'Oh really! Then come to my cabin when you are free. Let's talk about it in detail. But on one condition, please come with your single face. By the way, these ten faces look better on you than the two faces,' joked PK and both laughed.

'Congrats bro,' a random employee wished Karthik.

'Thank you but it's our team effort. I helped them only in procuring the items,' acted Karthik as if he is modest.

'No bro. Didn't you check the mail? You have won second prize in the solo variety talent event.'

'Really? I couldn't believe it,' grinned Karthik, not knowing how to react.

Wishes poured in for Karthik and Rini was more delighted than Karthik himself. Praveen Kumar became unsettled, as he felt that he should have been the person to tell good news.

'Bloody bugger, stole my thunder,' muttered PK. He thought for a moment and announced, 'Also wait for another good news. Ha Ha,' to gain their attention and the team were puzzled.

'Has Rini won the first prize?' asked Karthik.

'Are you referring to the bay decoration PK?' guessed Aysha and the teammates looked at him with curiosity.

'No, No, No! It's confidential. I won't reveal the winners now,' PK left the bay along with the organising committee.

The teammates chattered once he left and assumed that based on the judge's impression, they should at least get 3rd prize.

'Whatever may be the result. You guys pulled it off well and great job Aysha, you managed it with a lot of ease,' appreciated Jagan.

All of a sudden, the teammates spotted Praveen Kumar rushing back to their bay, ensuring no one is behind him, as if someone is chasing him to murder.

'I unofficially announce that your team is the winner of the bay decoration competition, but don't tell anyone until you receive an official announcement,' and the teammates jumped for joy.

While returning after the announcement, he found the random employee who stole his thunder by congratulating and announcing the second prize news to Karthik. 'You gave second prize, but I gave them first prize. I won,' fist pumped PK and the random employee scratched his head seeing him walk away with much pride.

*

CHAPTER 7 – DIM SPOT AND ROOMIES

As Kavita entered the cubicle, she felt the place was gloomy and looked around to notice that the lights above her were not switched on.

'I think it will rain today, it's so dark,' commented Karthik.

'Hey! the lights are switched off,' clarified Kavita.

'You mean the sunlight?'

Kavita gave a deadly stare.

'Calm down. I tried to live the life of Chocku for a moment.'

'Don't even try. It results in brain fever.'

'For who him or others? Wait let me go and check.'

Strolled to the switch board and found all the lights to be switched on. He tried switching off and on, but still doesn't work.

'Kavita, only those lights are not working. There should be a problem in one line. Let me go inform the admin.'

'No. I like this lighting. It sets up a pleasant mood. You too try working in this atmosphere. I am pretty sure you will like it. Let them repair it when they find it themselves.'

'I can adapt to any situation,' said Karthik

Chocku walked into the bay and stopped for a moment. Closed his left eye and found the room dark, then closed his right eye to find the room bright. He thought it's because of not wearing glasses today. He felt inferior by the fact that his eyesight is weak and doesn't want the teammates to know about it.

'Why are you dancing Bharatanatyam in the middle of the bay?' asked Karthik as it looked like Chocku highlighting his eyes with his fingers.

'Isn't one side brighter than before?'

'How can one think of an obvious thing from a different angle with such spontaneity?' wondered Karthik as ideally one should have asked *why one side is darker than before?* with the hand on his chin. 'Yeah, there is an extra bulb on your side,' mocked Karthik.

'Oh okay.'

'Chocku what is the speed of light?' Kavita questioned.

'299 792 458 metres per second,' replied in $4*10^8$ metres per second

'What's the use? All the knowledge goes to his recycle bin,' mumbled Kavita.

'But I like this ambience. The admin has good aesthetic sense,' remarked Chocku.

'True. Isn't it so comfy? I am glad we share the same feeling.'

Vinoth entered the bay and asked, 'Why is it so dark?

'Think it will rain today,' said Chocku.

Vinoth looked up to notice the light was switched off.

'No, the light has gone.'

'You mean the sunlight?'

'Chocku Why?' stressed Vinoth. 'There should be some problem with the bulb or line.'

'No, they have installed an extra bulb on one side,' pointed up without looking.

'Did you look at the other side?'

'No, it's glaring to see the lights,' hesitated Chocku as he didn't want him to know that he has poor eyesight.

'For God's sake see up once and then talk. Once, just once.'

'Yesss,' frustrated Chocku. 'I have poor eyesight and I can't see when I don't wear glasses. I have -4 power. Are you happy now? What gives you happiness in pinpointing someone's weakness.'

All three looked at Chocku going out of the hall with a confused face.

'I don't even remember him wearing spectacles in the first place,' confused Vinoth

*

When Karthik was on a phone call outside the ODC, he was looking through the window to find Aysha and Rini coming together in Rini's motorbike which is unusual as Aysha used to come by bus. As the lift opened, Karthik disconnected his call and enquired about it.

'Hey how come you both are coming together?' questioned Karthik as they walked towards the bay.

'We are best friends. Why shouldn't we come together?'

'Yes, you both are best friends,' nodded his head with so much hesitation as he doesn't trust girls who explicitly express their friendship, since he had come across such friends who criticise behind their back. 'I actually meant, you both come from different routes, right? Did your best friend pick you up on the way?' sarcastically said Karthik.

'Not only best friends,' said Rini.

'What?' shocked Karthik.

'No idiot. We are roomies,' both put their hands over one another's shoulder.

'Wow! When did this happen? You never told me. Finally, you found a roommate. Your dad must be happy now.'

'Yes,' relieved Rini.

'I shifted during the weekend. It was a sudden plan. It's very tiring for me to travel as it takes nearly 2 hours to reach the office,' expressed Aysha, as if even talking about it makes her tired.

'Okay, but reconsider your decision. Didn't you get any other roomie?' looked at Rini and smirked. Rini tapped on his bag.

'No way. She gave me full support in shifting the things and arranging them in the room. She took so much more care than I expected,' Aysha embraced her over the hip.

'You do all sorts of work except office work and that too only during weekends.'

'I do it on weekdays too.'

'You mean other than office work?'

'Hey, not another word about my roomie again,' Aysha warned Karthik by pointing her finger. 'And why is the bay looking dark?'

'Yeah,' acknowledged Rini.

'It symbolically conveys *dark days ahead* for you two,' commented Karthik.

'Get lost. We are going to have some great fun together,' both enacted some weird gesture. 'This is our roomie way of greeting each other,' said Aysha.

'First symptom of Rini infection.', teased Karthik

*

Jagan inspected the tracker and found that the productivity of the team is less than usual. 'Come,' pinged Jagan. Vinoth, who was in the meeting room, checked the message and came to the seat worried.

'Why is productivity low today? Are they working?' asked Jagan in a furious manner.

'No,' replied Vinoth.

'How dare you? If they aren't working? Tell them to work, man.'

'No Jagan. I mean, I didn't check whether they are working or not.'

'Isn't that your only work?'

'Too many issues are going on and I had to attend a lot of meetings, so I couldn't focus on them.'

'If you keep on attending only meetings, then when will you work? Let's sort it out. Tell me the issues now.'

'E&B Italy issue, KDMG UK issue, Bulb issue.'

'Bulb issue?' garbled Jagan.

'The lights are not working on one side of the bay, so I had to check with the admin.'

'Oh okay. The entrance door is making some screeching noise, can you ask the admin to oil it?'

'Will do it immediately Jagan.'

'Fool. Learn to prioritise your work.'

'Sorry. Let me ask him to first solve the bulb and then ask him to oil the door.'

'Idiot, now go and check the reason for low productivity,' hurled Jagan, and Vinoth rushed to the bay to check on his teammates.

"We all are going through Nyctophilia,' Chocku sounded as if he was talking while getting a Thai massage.

'What's Nyctophilia?' asked Karthik.

'Love of darkness; finding relaxation and comfort in the darkness,' defined Chocku in a breezy voice

'You would get that comfort even if you don't wear your spectacles.', commented Karthik

Chocku became furious as he made comment about his eye sight. He slowly came forward from his push back seat and looked intensely at Karthik, but actually there was no one in that direction. Meanwhile, Vinoth entered the bay and found everyone sitting in the dark corner.

'What are you people doing out there? Is this the reason for the low productivity today? Do you want me to keep a tab on you all the time like kids? If you guys don't finish the assigned task today, then the consequences will be bad,' warned Vinoth and as he moved closer to the dark place, he calmed down unconsciously and his voice tone changed. 'Now, everybody back to your work. I have informed the admin to fix the light. They will come now,' said as if he was hypnotised.

Everyone left the area unwillingly as if the vampires were asked to expose in sunlight.

'Vinoth, I have an alternate solution. Let's switch off all the lights to make it even,' said Chocku

'Even then you will be odd,'

'Dare not comment about my eye sight again,' fumed Chocku and left to his seat, but sat on Karthik's lap

Vinoth was confused, as he referred to his character as odd and not eye sight

*

Rini and Karthik were in the canteen sipping coffee, but Rini was pondering about something holding the steaming coffee that caressed her face. Karthik found her behavior quite different.

'Are you facing any financial problem?'

'No, why?'

'Then why do you take a steam facial with a free cup of coffee?'

'Hey No. I was thinking whether to share my problems with you.'

'Feel free to share. About whom do you want to complaint?'

'How can you think that I am going to complaint about her. How judgemental?'

'Her? So, tell me who she is?'

Sheepishly smiled and said, 'Aysha.'

'Oh, your roomie!' smirked Karthik.

'Hey but please don't judge. I really like her so much, but we both are not compatible as roommates.'

'Okay! What's the problem?'

'She takes 1.5 hours to take a bath and we have only one rest room.'

'1.5 hours? 90 minutes. I am saving 88 minutes of my life.'

'And while sleeping, she is not switching off the room light. I even politely asked her, but she was not willing and I couldn't force her too. I am not getting any sleep at all.'

'But why?' Karthik was confused.

'Her reason was weird. She said, anyways it's dark when we close our eyes, then why do we have to switch off the light. I was like, is it really Aysha who is giving such dumb reasons. Had Graham Bell been alive, he would have voluntarily died out of electric shock after inventing it.'

'Graham bell invented the telephone, not electricity.'

'Whoever it is. Don't you understand my pain?'

'Yes, I do. Thank God! She didn't ask me who invented electricity,' muttered Karthik.

'Though I was feeling lonely, I was happily eating outside in my favourite hotels in and around my house. She said that she will cook for both of us, so that we can save money.'

'Isn't that a good decision?'

'I couldn't even take it near my mouth. I directly feed it in my throat without touching the tongue. I am afraid we will get into an argument if I talk about all this to her.'

'Hi roomieee..,' greeted Aysha with excitement.

'Hi Roomieee..,' hugged Rini and then they both gestured their roommate's signature move and Karthik couldn't tolerate the drama.

'Shall we do something refreshing today?' asked Aysha.

'You must be tired cooking. Why not buy pizza?'

'No way. I will cook you homemade pizza today.'

"Okay then let's go out to purchase ingredients this evening," replied Rini with no sign of disinterest as she couldn't express her thoughts boldly considering her good relationship with her.

'Homemade Pizza,' Aysha hugged Rini.

'Yay!' Rini cried looking at Karthik.

*

Everyone in the office has left and the security Velumani is going around to check. He heard a snoring sound and traced the noise. He went near the person and woke him up and it's Vinoth sleeping in Kavita's seat. He woke up by wiping the saliva drooling over his mouth and looked around, mesmerised by the darkness.

Then took his bag and left the place, but he didn't want to go as he had the best sleep.

*

Next morning, Karthik was hesitant to ask Aysha for a break to talk about the issue Rini is facing with her in the room. He then gathered courage and when he was about to ask her, Aysha asked Karthik for a break to his surprise.

'You usually don't ask for a break. You too have something to say?'

'You too want to tell me something?'

'Yes, but feminist first,' kidded Karthik and they both went to the canteen.

Karthik was wondering what it could be and after a few moments of pause, Aysha said, 'I am finding it difficult to be roommates with Rini.'

'Have I got into a loop? I keep hearing the same thing,' Karthik told himself. 'Why? What's the problem?'

'She is not at all disciplined,' came closer and said, 'She didn't even bathe today.'

'What?' shocked Karthik. 'You knew it only now? The whole team knew it well before.'

'She heavily snores and I am scared to hear it when the lights are off. It sounds weird and uneven. The moment she sleeps, her snore creeps in. It's like she closes her eyes, keeps the snore device on her head and makes noise like an ambulance throughout the night. So, I sleep without switching off the light, hiding the actual reason.'

'Father of electricity will be happy now,' relieved Karthik.

'Who is the father of electricity?' asked Aysha.

'Graham bell did not discover electricity.'

'I only voluntarily asked her that we shall cook to save some money, but she is not even helping me in washing the vessels. At times I make some simple dishes, so that I don't need to wash many vessels.'

'Hey, why didn't you guys call me for a break?' interrupted Rini.

'Do you know what the distance of smell is?'

'Distance of smell?'

'Yes. Please find it and maintain that distance here on.'

'Hey get lost' and does the roomie signature move with Aysha.

For each move they do, the words from his mind, made a move towards his mouth and shouted,

'Stop it' and looked at Rini. 'Since you are snoring in a horrific manner, she is afraid to switch off the lights.'

Then he looked at Aysha, 'And you are taking a bath for more than an hour and that is why she is not getting time to bath.'

Again, pointed out Rini, 'You are not helping her in washing the vessels and that is why she is cooking with disinterest.'

Now towards Aysha again, 'She hates your food,' and again turned towards Rini but had nothing to say.

The whole canteen became silent for an instant. The coffee stopped dripping from the machine, the red ants froze as if they caught red handed stealing the samosa, a middle-aged employee who was about to fart in the buzz of conversation put it on hold.

Rini and Aysha, looked at each other with awkward reactions.

'Do I snore Aysha? No one has ever told me that.'

'Do I take a long time to bathe? I haven't realised it before, since I have always been at home and not in hostel.'

'I can sleep on the veranda if my snoring is loud. There is enough space to sleep.'

'No, I shall keep cotton in my ears. And I will not take much time to bathe again.'

'I will wash the vessel.'

'No, we shall hire a cook,' and both compromised by hugging each other.

'You are my best roomie,' said Rini and they gestured their roomie moves.

Stared at them for a moment and abruptly said, 'Can you guys teach me too?'.

They taught him to do the gesture and the middle-aged employee farted peacefully ever after.

*

Vinoth relished his sleep at Kavita's desk last night and he wished to take over her desk.

'Kavita, can you move to my desk until the lights are fixed? My desk would be spacious, brighter and comfortable for you.'

'No Vinoth. I will be here. It's not a big concern for me.'

'No. Trust me. There is a reason behind everything I say. It's for the betterment of your work.'

The lights get switched on as they talk. Kavita is disappointed as the lights are fixed. Vinoth thinks that there is no purpose to move to her desk now.

'Okay forget it. You be there. Our team comfort comes first to me.'

They all heard someone snoring and they traced the noise to see Rini sleeping in the bay. Aysha became afraid and went near Karthik.

Jagan walked to the bay hearing the noise and asked, 'What noise is that? Vinoth, have you started repairing the grinder in the bay?' and then looked at Rini. 'Empty vessel making the loudest noise,' commented Jagan.

Chocku assumed that Vinoth had been caught red handed for sleeping in the bay, as he couldn't identify who it was properly. 'You deserve for teasing about my eyesight,' Chocku told himself. He wasn't sure where Jagan was standing and figured out that someone was standing adjacent to him and asked, 'Where is Jagan?' to Jagan himself.

*

CHAPTER 8 – FRIGHT FRIDAY AND COOL TRANSFER

It's Friday evening 6 pm and the situation looked quite worrisome. Jagan was stressed out pinching out his beard and Vinoth was restless, biting his nail.

'This is a very tough situation. We have to handle it with much care,' Jagan advised Vinoth.

'Why should we face the troubles for no mistake of ours. This is the moment I hate the most in my life.'

'It's part and parcel of our life. Be stone hearted and we don't have much time. Sooner the better.'

'I was happy while coming to the office as today is Friday,' muttered Vinoth and left the room.

He went to his desk, took his bag and left the office without even making eye contact with anyone.

'Why is he leaving early today? Would he allow me to go if I leave so early?' Kavita told herself and asked, 'Vinoth why are you leaving early today?'

'It will come soon.'

'What will come?'

'Ah Ahem Wife!' words fumbled.

'Why do you address your wife like an object?'

'Sorry. I told by mistake. I have to pick her up. Happy Weekend. See you on Monday,' controlled his tears. He then peeped at the manager's room while crossing and found an empty chair rolling as if Jagan had launched himself from the chair to his home.

'Hey we have received mail from HR. Oh its appraisal mail,' informed Rini.

'What? Appraisal mail?' panicked Kavita.

'The ratings are out?' feared Karthik.

'Oh my god,' Aysha checked the mail with curiosity.

Karthik checked to know that he has got 3rd rating. 1 is the highest and 4th is the least. He was neither sad nor happy about it.

Rini came to Karthik's seat and asked, 'Hey what's your rating?'

'3rd'

'Lol. You worked your ass off for this?' kidded Rini.

'What's yours?' asked Karthik nervously as she was worried whether Rini has got a better rating than him.

'4th rating,' laughed Rini.

'Even the one who has got 1st rating wouldn't be happy like you.'

'Come let's go check out what others have got.'

'Hey one shouldn't ask the rating explicitly.'

'Rini, I have been promoted,' Aysha informed Rini.

'Vow roomie,' Rini opened her arms and they hugged each other.

'You have suffered a lot to achieve this. They must have given you for achieving the targets despite being roommates with Rini.'

'Hey, I am a lucky charm.'

'So, what's your rating guys?' asked Aysha.

'Me 3rd. Tell yours Miss Lucky charm.'

'4th,' Rini said in a casual manner.

'Rini worked really hard but Aysha isn't a lucky charm,' teased Karthik.

'I expected 4th and I got the same. I have met the expectation,' Rini and Aysha laughed together.

'It upsets me seeing you behaving cool even in this situation. I wouldn't be this upset, had I even got 4th rating,' Karthik banged his head.

'Hey! Kavita looks dull. Think she isn't satisfied with the rating,' remarked Aysha.

All three went to her place to console her and she was seen lying down on the table. Aysha sat beside her and kept her hands on the shoulder. Kavita woke up and wiped her tears. She began to talk even before Aysha asked her anything.

'I expected promotion at least this time. It's been 8 years,' cried Kavita.

Aysha pacified her by caressing her shoulder.

'You demand Vinoth to promote by stating all your achievements'

'He has left. And I am not sure whether I will have the same anger on Monday. Also, I feel hopeless.'

'Now I know why the management releases the rating on Friday EOD,' Aysha shook her head.

'Push yourself because no one else is going to do it for you,' motivated Rini.

Rini and Karthik gestured to Aysha to take care of her and moved on to Chocku's desk to know his rating.

'What is your rating Chocku,' asked Rini.

'Rating should not be revealed.'

Rini and Karthik moved aside and discussed a plan to know his rating and then stood at a minimal distance to ensure he heard their conversation.

'Chocku should have got 1st rating,' commented Karthik as if he was having a casual chat.

Chocku angrily looked at Karthik and when Karthik looked at him, he immediately turned away to the monitor like the trains in theme park taking an abrupt turn with the rails.

'No, I think he might have got 3rd rating,' replied Rini.

'Why did you miss 4th, assume that too,' yelled Chocku.

'So, we both have got the same rating?'

'What? You too got 2nd rating?'

'Mission completed, come let's go,' left Rini and Karthik.

*

It's Monday morning and the office looked like a chosen war field which is going to see a lot of blood sheds. Chocku entered the office and shivered as he took his seat and switched on the computer.

'These guys knew that I am angry and trying to make me cool by reducing the AC temperature. I am not going to fall for this,' Chocku told himself. Then he calmed down by considering that let this be a rehearsal for him to survive onsite, where the temperature is always in minus. But as the time passed, he stood up, 'No I don't want onsite opportunity,' murmured as he walked to the admin's room.

'It's so cold inside, can you please increase the temperature?', complained Chocku

'We are maintaining the same temperature limit like any other day and no one has complained about it,' said a young guy from the admin team.

'Consider the temperature of the outside atmosphere too. It's so cold outside. Haven't you learnt about heat transfer through convection? '

The admin member became heated up to an extent that the cool atmosphere would become warm.

'The sound of keyboard typing is in synchrony with my teeth chattering. It's that cold.'

'Okay I will increase it,' nodded the admin guy.

Meanwhile, Aysha at her desk felt that it's so sweaty inside and stood in front of AC to check if AC is functioning. She felt her mind was disturbed by it and couldn't peacefully enjoy her promotion phase, so she too went to report to the admin.

'Can you please lower the temperature? It's so hot inside,' complained Aysha.

'Due to heat transfer through convection, the office is naturally cool it seems, so I had to increase the temperature.'

'Which crackpot told you? Wait. Is it Chockalingam?'

'I don't know his name, but if you find someone whose teeth chattering is in synchrony with keyboard typing then it's him.'

'I will see to it. You can lower the temperature.'

Chocku felt cold again and went to the admin room.

'It's still, very cold boss.'

'I got a complaint that it's too hot in there.'

'From whom?'

'Aysha madam. You please discuss with her and come to a conclusion.'

'What's the use of getting 1st rating? Doesn't even know about the concept of heat transfer,' fumed Chocku.

*

Vinoth walked cautiously to his desk and greeted good morning in hesitation, which came out from his mouth in the next appraisal. Kavita didn't respond, but once he took his seat she came to his desk and said, 'I need to discuss with you regarding my appraisal.'

'Sure,' stammered Vinoth. We have planned for a feedback session at 11 am, we shall discuss at that time.

'Okay,' left Kavita controlling her nerves.

Vinoth made a call to his wife. 'Just wanted to say take care. Not sure whether I will make to home today.'

*

It's 11 am, Vinoth and Jagan are at the other end of the table in Jagan's room, ready to conduct the feedback session.

Rini walked inside angrily and sat on the chair.

'Yes Rini, what do you feel about your rating?' asked Jagan.

'I am very disappointed.'

'Yes, we too are disappointed.'

'What didn't I do?'

'You didn't work'

'I was willing to work, but you never allocated me proper work. That's your mistake. This company doesn't deserve me. I am going to put on my papers.'

Vinoth and Jagan felt happy about it and looked at each other controlling their joy, but their eyes expressed their happiness as their eye ball turned into a smiley ball.

'No, don't take such a decision. We can equip you and make you a better resource. You have got that potential in you.'

'Okay. Learn to get the work done,' ordered Rini and exited the room.

'Did she give advice to us?' Jagan asked Vinoth in confusion.

'Will be right back Jagan. I need to go to the restroom,' fearing about other teammates as even the non-performer Rini is commanding them and he imagined about others who performed well, but dissatisfied with the rating.

'I would better save it for the best,' mumbled Jagan.

*

Chocku walked directly towards Aysha. He wanted to walk in a threatening manner, but the shiver in his body wasn't allowing him to do so.

'Aysha, why did you ask him to reduce the temperature? I feel cold.'

'I feel warm.'

Then there is a moment of silence between them before Chocku's teeth start chattering again.

'Okay fine. Let's get votes from our teammates and decide based on the majority.', said Aysha

'The teammates' mood is spoiled after appraisal. We can't go now and quarrel like you do, to get votes.'

'Our motive is to know whether they feel cold or not, but they shouldn't know we are there to get votes.'

Chocku agreed to her suggestion. First, they went to get vote from Kavita.

'Don't keep on thinking about appraisal Kavita. Keep yourself *warm*,' Chocku stressed on the last phrase.

'Something better is awaiting to *cool* your mind,' said Aysha.

'Is it so?'

'You are already upset and it's cold too. Why do they lower the temperature when someone is upset,' Chocku triggered the curiosity of Kavita.

'So what?'

'Don't you know that coldness aggravates depression? The climate in Greenland is always in minus degree Celsius and the suicidal rate is very high in Greenland.'

'This is not cool Chocku. This will trouble her,' said Aysha as she could feel Chocku is on the verge of gaining her vote.

'No, I am feeling cold. For my current state of mind, I may do something foolish. It's better to increase the temperature'

'Chocku 1, Aysha 0,' said Chocku, and Kavita overheard it.

'No, Kavita is zero. All my hard work has gone waste,' Kavita started to whine about her appraisal again and both left to gather votes from others.

*

Now it's Aysha's turn for a feedback session. She went to the room and Jagan was standing behind his chair facing the wall waiting for Vinoth to come from the restroom. He turned and asked her to take the seat and started the session.

'We are highly satisfied with your performance and my hearty congratulations.' Jagan expressed by resting his hand on the chair standing behind.

Thanks to you Jagan. I wouldn't have achieved this without your guidance.'

Vinoth came back from restroom

'I know. Going forward, you should take more responsibilities, learn new technologies and upscale your skills. One should work with passion and dedication to reach this place,' Jagan pointed his chair.

Vinoth sat on the chair Jagan pointed. Vinoth realised he had sat on the wrong chair and moved to his chair.

'And why aren't you not participating in extra-curricular activities like before. That too is equally important'

'Since I have back pain, the doctor has advised me to quit Bharatanatyam, but I am going to singing classes now. In the future, I will probably participate in a singing competition.

'Vinoth too is good with musical instruments.'

'Yes, I am well aware of it,' controlled her laugh as she got reminded of *Jalra*

'You both can even perform together in future events.'

'No, that instrument won't go well with me.'

'What?'

'I mean Guitar, because I am a classical singer.'

'So what? He can learn musical instrument technology too,' laughed by patting Vinoth's shoulder.

'Yes Jagan,' nodded Vinoth.

'He is playing it well. Sorry! He can learn to play it well too.'

She then thanked both of them and came out to join Chocku in getting votes from Karthik.

*

'Why are you in deep thought Karthik?' asked Aysha.

'Are you thinking about lowering the AC temperature?' asked Chocku.

'No.'

'Yeah, why does he have to think about it when the temperature is optimal,' snubbed Aysha.

'I am just worried whether I really have potential to work here.'

'Why do you underestimate yourself? You will figure it out gradually. I haven't seen you like this before. Aren't you a *Chilled* out person?' emphasised Aysha.

'Yes.'

'Aren't you a cool-headed guy?'

'Yes.'

'Do you want this place to be as cool as you?'

'Yes.'

'Good. Thank you,' left Aysha even before he realised what he said 'Yes' to and Chocku ran behind her.

'This is not fair. You are playing mind games. He said it in a flow without consciousness.'

'Never mind. 1 each now.'

'You are cold hearted.'

*

Now it's Karthik's turn for the feedback session. He stopped near the door and told himself to be calm and composed before getting inside the room.

'Yes, Karthik, what do you feel about the rating?' asked Jagan, and both were a bit worried inside as to how he was going to react.

'I feel I got what I deserved.'

Vinoth and Jagan were shocked and at the same time very much relieved to get such an answer from him.

'You deserve 2nd rating, but the master table deletion issue had a financial impact for the client.'

'I understand.'

'It's evident that you are giving your best, but technically you have to upskill'

'Yes, it's not getting into my head despite putting in a lot of effort, but yeah I will improve soon.'

'Do you have any questions?' in a most pleasing manner.

'No Jagan. I am all good.'

'Vinoth, please drop him in his seat,' his voice broke down in emotion as he felt gifted to have such a appraisal friendly member in his team

'Okay Jagan, will drop and let you know.'

'Karthik opened the door and when he was about to close it, Jagan stopped him.'

'Would you have given the same answer had you got 4th rating?'

'May be.'

'Shall we change it now then?'

'Jagan!' shocked Karthik.

'Ha-ha! That was a joke', managed Jagan and once Karthik left, 'Too late. Missed it!' Jagan banged on the table.

*

Aysha and Chocku approached Rini while she was working with earphones plugged in, her legs were on the chair folded and was rocking her head to *Naatu Naatu song from RRR*. She then unplugged as they went near her.

'Rini, aren't you sad for getting 2nd rating,' asked Chocku as he thought she too got the same rating as him based on the conversation they had when she came with Karthik.

Aysha and Rini laughed as he was unaware about her actual rating.

'As long as you are there, I will not be worried about anything'

'Nothing can affect my roomie,' hugged Aysha.

'Exactly. In what angle do I look sad? I don't even require AC.'

Aysha suddenly took her hands off Rini, 'Why did you say that?' stunned Aysha because that phrase nearly qualifies Chocku to gain the vote.

'Because I am a chilled-out person then why do I need an AC,' laughed Rini.

Now, Chocku laughed along with her and said 'Karma is faster than I expected!' Chocku thanked looking up. 'This is the first time, you make sense to me Rini,' and both walked away. As they were walking, Chocku was moving in reverse happily humming *Naatu Naatu,* but gesturing *Nought Nought Nought* to Aysha symbolically conveying that he won.

'Too early to celebrate. Vinoth and Jagan are still pending.'

'I am not on good terms with them after appraisal.'

'I thought you must have got 1st rating. I am sorry Chocku.'

'Will you lower the temperature based on empathy then?'

'No. I don't mix empathy on one matter to another. The temperature elction is still on.'

'I will be back after my feedback session,' Chocku went to the room.

*

Jagan and Vinoth waited for Chocku for quite some time, but he hasn't shown up yet.

'What has he got in store for us today?' worried Vinoth.

'We have to speak according to his mood,' advised Jagan.

'Why is he taking so much time? You go and check him out.'

Vinoth went and found him just outside the door, leaning on the wall facing outside. He then immediately pulled his head back inside to inform Jagan.

'Jagan he is standing just outside the room, but I am not sure why he isn't getting inside.'

'I understood. He is angry at us, so he feels disinterested to ask us *May I come in?*. Now wait and watch.'

'May you please come?'

Chocku entered without uttering a word, took his seat and looked away from them. Jagan gestured to Vinoth to calm down and initiated the conversation.

'One point was reduced because..'

'They have always been reducing. When have they increased?'

'They? Who are they?'

'The Admin. Still, they haven't reduced the temperature.'

'Vinoth please go check why the admin has not increased the temperature. I don't want to see Chocku being uncomfortable.'

'Nooooo,' a loud noise came from nowhere and they wondered Why? And Who? is shouting. It was Aysha, the loser, who shouted as she overheard the conversation inside.

Chocku knew it was Aysha and he fist pumped since he got both their votes in one go.

'Reducing it is my responsibility Chocku,' assured Vinoth.

'Yes, you are responsible,' Chocku accused him.

'I am yet to tell the admin.'

'I think now he is talking about his rating,' whispered Jagan into the ears of Vinoth.

'Why am I not given 1st rating? I have completed all the tasks within the promised deadline without any escalation. Then why?'

'Instead, we will get you onsite opportunity,' said Jagan.

'Onsite? No, I can't bear the climate.'

'We will plan a package during summer season with complimentary breakfast.'

'You can go and chill out there.'

'Chill?' came forward from his seat.

'No! Work hard, sweat hard, persevere and perspire, Okay?'

'That's convincing. I hope you keep up the promise.'

*

The feedback session has reached its most crucial phase. Next is Kavita and they are unsure about how to convince her.

'What shall we do now Jagan?' trembled Vinoth.

'The time has come. Let me go to the restroom and you will be here until I come back.'

Vinoth was nervous of facing Kavita alone, and sat there like a kid waiting for the parent to come out from the public toilet worried whether they would abandon them. To his dismay Kavita came inside. He stood from his seat in anxiety as if the income tax officer made a surprise raid at his home. Then he asked her to sit, but even her mind did not emit a thought to utter a word.

'Let's wait for Jagan to come. He has gone to the restroom,' informed Vinoth and then they remained silent. She ignored him to an extent that even the air she breathed out did not go to his side. Though they were in the same room, Vinoth felt like they were several light years away. 2 mins of Kavita felt like 20 years for Vinoth. After a few minutes Jagan was back and started the session.

'What do you feel about your rating Kavita?'

'I expected promotion this cycle Jagan. It's been 8 years since I have been promoted,' her voice broke.

'Please don't cry,' Vinoth appeased her.

'How do you expect me to take it, Vinoth. We both joined in the same year, but I haven't got the promotion. Not that I am comparing myself with you, but I deserve promotion at least now. I have been honest to my work and you both know that. I am doing the best I could amidst the household work. I wake up in the morning at 5 am. It takes 2 hours of effort to cook breakfast and lunch. 30 mins of effort to bathe my kid. 1 to 2 hours of effort to feed my kid and he never eats if my husband feeds him. Then I have to travel 45 mins to reach the office and work for 8 hours despite being dog tired. Again, I have to travel 45 mins to reach home, 1 hour effort to cook dinner and 1 hour effort to put my kid to sleep. Above all, he wakes me up at least thrice in the middle of the night.

'None of the efforts you mentioned are related to the office.'

'Jagan, her husband is not earning. He has been trying to crack UPSC exams for years. She is the only income to her family. Though she hasn't exceeded our expectation, she has indeed met the expectation,' added Vinoth.

'You can't recommend her for emotional reasons, Vinoth. I want numbers. The management will not consider these emotional factors. Kavita, we also wanted to promote you, but a guy from the AWS team has outperformed you and the management has decided to give it to him.'

'Okay Jagan. Sorry that I vented out my personal problems here. I know it's not just me and everyone has their own personal problems.'

'As per the quota allocated to us, we aren't able to give you. Myself and Vinoth tried our best.'

'Okay, I will work harder than before Jagan. Thanks, Vinoth,' deserted Kavita with a frown face, knowing that she has to accept and move on.

'Okay Vinoth, how do you feel?' asked Jagan.

'I am feeling very bad, Jagan. Is there any possibility to try again?'

'Hey I asked how you feel about your rating man?'

'Oh Sorry! Now that's not even a concern to me.'

*

Aysha admitted her defeat and agreed to increase the temperature. They both go to the admin room to inform.

'You can increase the AC temperature now,' said Aysha to the admin

'You guys are pretty sure? Have you calculated the heat transfer equations?'

'If you talk too much, mass transfer will take place. We will report and transfer you,' replied Chocku.

'HaHa! If you report me for *talking too much*, then it's like laying your own trap,' kidded the admin guy.

Chocku was enraged with his counter, but since Aysha laughed it diluted his anger and he too disguised like enjoying it by putting up a mixed reaction, as if both heat and mass transfer were occurring simultaneously on his face.

*

Kavita eyes was locked on the blinking cursor with hands on the keyboard without typing. The mail popped up in her computer and snapped her mind to consciousness. Her eyes skimmed through the mail and her face glowed. Her eyes sucked the tears that poured out and she started to make some squeaking noises out of joy with both the hands on her mouth as she couldn't believe what she just read. Vinoth look her at from far and shook his head in distress thinking that she was weeping. With happy tears in her eyes, she stood and advanced towards Vinoth, but seeing tears in her eyes he prepared his mind for round 2.

Thank you so much Vinoth. I just received the promotion mail,' smiled Kavita.

'Are you serious?' he stood out of astonishment and congratulated aloud, shaking her hands.

Everyone in the bay became elated and conveyed their wishes.

'Thank you once again Vinoth'

'I am not even aware of this. You should thank Jagan.'

Jagan then cut in the middle of celebration and said, 'Congrats Kavita. I have fought with HR to get you promoted. To say it in your style, 2 hours of effort to fight with HR.'

'Means a lot, Jagan.'

'Why didn't you inform me about this Jagan?' enquired Vinoth.

'Only then, when Kavita ask you about it, you would reply *You should be thankful to Jagan,*' kidded Jagan.

Everyone laughed wholeheartedly for the first time to Jagan's comment.

'Hot news - Teammates in Micron Tech laughed for a manager's joke,' teased Karthik, and everyone laughed including Jagan, but deep inside he suspected whether he was being mocked for giving 3rd rating to Karthik.

'Since you said hot news, isn't it hot today guys?' said Aysha, and smiled at Chocku.

Yeah, it's a bit warm today, right? We should inform the admin to reduce the temperature,' said Kavita, and Chocku gave up since everyone unanimously agreed. 'Okay, let's inform the admin and go for a break. It's my treat.'

'You can't get away by giving treat in the canteen. This is a trial treat,' replied Vinoth and while everyone were getting out of the ODC,

'Get me a seat near the boiler,' said Chocku.

The whole team stood in front of the admin's room which is on the way to the canteen. The admin was under the table looking for his pen and got up to see everyone standing in front of him.

'When will I get promotion?' cried admin, so that he could break free from this role.

*

CHAPTER 9 – TAX FILING AND HEART BLOCKS

Karthik, while looking at today's date on his system, he knew he had marked something to do on this day, so he checked his sticky notes to find that today is the last day for filing income tax declaration. He was terrified and informed everyone. They are in shock because none of them have filed. Chocku did not utter a word though he had completed, since they would ask help from him to fill it on behalf of them. But that couldn't help because now everyone is in front of Chocku pleading to fill it. He tried to convince everyone to do it on their own as it's very simple, but they aren't willing to do it.

'Since I have got promotion, you have to guide me to invest in a lot of stuff,' requested Kavita to Chocku.

'Invest some in humility too,' replied Vinoth, and Kavita smiled sheepishly.

Rini has no clue about it and was least worried as her dad would file ITR through form 16 later even if she doesn't declare now and submit the actuals.

Meanwhile, Vinoth got a call and moved away from the crowd to attend it. While he was listening, he panicked and shivered, as his dad had been admitted in hospital after a severe attack.

'Guys, my dad has suffered an attack and he is in hospital. I have to leave now.'

The teammates are out of words to pacify him.

'Don't worry Vinoth, he will get well,' said Kavita.

'Let me know if you need any help,' said Karthik.

'Okay. Kavita, please take care of the UK kick start meeting at 4 pm and track the work of all our team tasks too.'

'Okay. You don't think anything about it. I will take care.'

Before leaving, he went to Jagan's room to inform him about the situation.

'You please go. Have you taken the life insurance card with you?' asked Jagan.

'Jagan!' Vinoth's BP had a sharp increase.

'Sorry! Sorry! Health insurance card,' calmed him down.

*

'Life is so unfair. I am now worried about my father. At least I shouldn't be a burden to him. Chocku, can you fill the declaration form on behalf of my dad?' requested Rini.

'What? But Vinoth has given me priority work.'

'Vinoth has asked me to take the responsibility, so I will manage it. You have to help us with this.'

'Okay I will teach you once,' but everyone pleaded again that they won't be able to get it.

'Stop. You people don't even know how to evade tax and call yourself educated. Who is coming first?'

Kavita came forward and took in-charge to organise it, 'I will tell you. A good team leader would give opportunity to their team members first,' said emotionally as she too wanted to get her process completed first. 'Karthik you first.'

Karthik sat beside Chocku.

'What's your gross amount?' asked Chocku.

'Monthly 3000.'

'Only 3000?' wondered Chocku.

'Yes, that's my grocery expense.'

'Not grocery idiot. I asked gross salary.'

'I don't know what the gross salary is, but my salary is 35000 per month.'

'That's CTC. Okay, at least tell me your net salary.'

'Do you get both gross salary and net salary? I get only one, no two salaries.'

'Shit,' bit his hand frustrated. 'You better show me your payslip.'

'Okay,' and opened his payslip.

'You have to submit the house rental and invest in any of these sections for 30000 to evade tax and submit your actuals later before the deadline.'

'Really? If I do this, they won't even collect tax in the toll booth?'

Chocku stared at him and Karthik realised he had said something really stupid and managed by saying.

'I just tried to behave like you for once.'

'Nexttt,' shouted Chocku.

*

'I think yours will be a love marriage,' said Rini.

'Me? Had I entered the expense I had spent in the matrimonial sites in 80C section, I would have easily evaded tax.'

'What's that 8th C? Sounds like a class section in school. I assume you studied in boys school and that's why your compatibility score with girls is low.'

'I doubt you went to school only till 8th C?. Submit your house rent proof and invest 25000 in any of these,' pinpointed the investment possibilities. 'I have filled the rest.'

'Will you do the investment too?'

'For the sake of giving birth to a daughter like you, your dad deserves to take the burden. Next,' shouted Chocku.

*

Vinoth rushed to the hospital and enquired about his dad in reception. He came to know that he was admitted in ICU and met his family members in the waiting room. The exact condition of his dad was unknown to anyone. Then he waited near the ICU for someone to come outside. A Nurse opened the door.

'Madam my dad's name is Ramkumar.'

'My dad's name is Shanmugam, please tell me,' said Nurse Mandhiravalli. A Senior Nurse who is older than Vinoth. Her tone sounded authoritative and posed a commanding appearance. Had she been in the army, the terrorist would dare not enter. The whole India would have been an ICU for her, India Care Unit. Even if the terrorist tries to bring in bombs, she would have hurled, 'Fruits not allowed inside ICU'.

'No. My dad is inside the ICU. Can I go see him?'

'He will be infected if you go inside. Not allowed now.'

'Okay, but at least check and let me know about his condition. I am his son.'

'Fine. Wait, I shall check and tell you.'

Nurse opened the door and Vinoth tried to look through the door to search for his dad. She went inside and sneaked out showing only her face and said, 'from here you will only be able to see patient Manimegalai.'

'Argh Okay! I won't see. Please go and check him.'

Vinoth was walking in the lobby impatiently and she came out after some time.

'We have taken an ECG and MRI scan. Now drips have been injected. Doctor will check the reports and tell you in detail. And before that, please get these medicines,' provided the sheet to him.

'Shall I go inside now?'

'Is everyone taking sun bath inside? There are other patients too. Wait until the doctor comes.'

Meanwhile, another person entered the ICU and she stopped him, 'Not allowed.'

'Hello, I am the doctor,' puts the coat on his shoulder.

'Sorry Doctor. You may go.'

Seeing all this, Vinoth is worried whether he will be able to see his dad crossing the stern Nurse.

*

Next on the line up is Aysha.

'Chocku, in recent days you haven't faced any issue with AC level, right? Because I ensured it doesn't exceed your level.'

'I have already accepted to fill the declaration form. Stop your drama'

'No, that's not the reason'

'Whatever, I am fed up with you guys. This Karthik fellow, doesn't even know what gross salary is.'

'Really?'

'What's your gross salary?'

'Can't you find it in my pay slip? It should be there, right?' and looked at the monitor seriously as if she knew.

'Best performer? You?'

'See, filling these forms are not in my roles and responsibilities.'

'So, is it my role and responsibilities? Do I have any use by filling these forms for you all? Can I add *I helped my teammates in filling the declaration form and filing ITR*? This is an individual's duty.'

'I don't know anything about this, but I can give you moral support.'

'Okay, go on.'

'I love you Chocku.'

'No that's wrong. Moral support means, one should say *Come on Chocku! Come on Chocku! you can do it.*'

'Not just moral support, I wish we share life support. I LOVE YOU,' she said those 3 words word by word with a gap, but emotionally was getting closer for every word. 'I don't know the moment I fell in love with you, but I do know you were seeping into my heart. Now, I want to share the overflowing love with you.'

Chocku, who has never ever been in such a situation, didn't know how to react.

'I only know to prevent integer overflow. I am not a subject matter expert in this topic.', panicked Chocku

'Yes, I will make you an expert.'

'Submit the house rent proof and invest Rs.40000 under 80C,' said his mind, but his heart beat has lost its rhythm.

'I have already invested and am expecting returns,' she looked into his eyes.

'In which hospital Vinoth's dad has been admitted? Think I need a bed,' said Chocku as if he was anaesthetised for a heart transplant.

Aysha left smiling and then Kavita took the seat.

'Kavita,' said Chocku keeping his mouth open, looking like a whale keeping it's mouth open to catch a shoal of fish.

'Gross salary, right? Gross Salary is employee provident fund EPF and gratuity subtracted from the Cost to Company. Net Salary = Gross Salary - Income Tax - Public Provident Fund- Professional Tax. Won't a team lead know such basic terminology.'

'What if she had heard the proposal?' mumbled Chocku and looked at her suspiciously.

Late evening, the teammates decided to go visit Vinoth's dad in hospital. They made arrangements for transportation with the vehicles they had and fortunately Aysha got onto Chocku's bike.

*

Vinoth came running and gave the medicines to the Nurse.

'Hope these medicines are only for my dad,' doubted Vinoth.

'The Nurse snatched and went inside without uttering a word thinking about his silliness. Vinoth then slowly opened the door to check out his dad, but found the Nurse still standing there gazing at him.

'I knew you would open again,' said Nurse Mandhiravalli.

'Argh. Please go give it to him madam' and after she went, 'she is one whole form of my teammates.', he grinded his teeth.

Vinoth then planned to go inside by standing close to the wall, so that when she comes out, he can slide in through the door from the side without knowing to her.

Teammates walked in the stairs towards the ICU and Jagan noticed Vinoth standing outside nervous, close to the wall like hiding from someone. The Nurse opened the door and Vinoth ran inside in a jiffy without getting caught in her eyes.

'Why is he playing ice spies with the Nurse?' Jagan told himself. He went to the Nurse and asked, 'Are you searching for Vinoth?'

'Yes.'

'The moment you came out, he went inside. He is a very timely person.'

'Aiyoh! I actually came out to allow him inside.'

'Shall we go now?'

'Only one person is allowed.'

Jagan turned to the teammates and informed, 'You guys be here. I will go and check him.'

'Mister, that one person has already gone inside. How are you related to them?'

'I am his boss.'

'You should not come here and ask for updates,' warned Mandhiravalli.

Vinoth came out and saw the teammates waiting near the ICU. Jagan enquired about the health condition and Vinoth informed the teammates as updated by the doctor that an angiogram has to be done and only based on the result, they can decide whether to perform by-pass surgery or place a stent.

'Fine. Don't worry. Glad he is safe now. My uncle had an attack and when he was about to cross the entrance, he passed aw....'

'Jagan!' Karthik grabbed his hand to stop him from saying anything negative now and he managed swiftly, 'He, He passed through several tests and it was just gas trouble,' he blinked.

'Thanks everyone for coming. It makes me feel better now.'

The teammates acknowledged and Chocku said, 'I have submitted the declaration form Vinoth.'

'Thank you Chocku.'

Jagan looked at Chocku in shock as he forgot to submit the declaration, 'Ah Chocku, I need your support for few minutes before you go home.'

'You too Brutax?. Next time I should collect additional tax for helping them fill it,' told himself.

*

Vinoth signalled Jagan to come in for a private chat and went to a side of the lobby. Meanwhile Chocku, 'Aysha can you please come here,' requested to come near the ICU door.

'There? Near the ICU?'

'Yeah, it's an emergency, so let's talk near the ICU.'

'Yes, tell me.'

'I don't want to prolong it anymore,' while he looked down in shyness, Nurse Mandhiravalli opened the door and came in between Chocku and Aysha.

'I LOVE YOU,' he said to Mandhiravalli. 'No, ICU ICU! Can I go inside,' he fumbled.

'Do you think I will allow, if you say *I Love You*. Even if you are my husband, I won't allow you inside.'

Aysha was on cloud nine that he had accepted and she rushed to Rini to whom she had already expressed her love for Chocku and whispered that Chocku had accepted. Rini felt overjoyed making noises, as if the ear phone was unplugged from the phone and Aysha calmed her down like plugging the ear phone back promptly.

'Jagan, I don't think I will continue working in IT. Probably will be taking care of my dad's business which is his wish too. You can start the hiring process for my replacement.', expressed Vinoth

'Okay Vinoth. But don't take any major decisions at this point. You can take your time and let me know later.'

'Everything will be alright,' and hugged Vinoth. Tears flowed down from Vinoth's eyes.

The teammates then left the hospital and while walking down the stairs, 'Guys in the upcoming days, we have to be more responsible since Vinoth will not be available for at least a month. Kavita, probably you will have to take his position. Aysha may be replacing Kavita's position. This is going to be a challenging phase', said Jagan.

'Jagan, since you have high hopes on us. I wanted to tell you this now, so that you can plan accordingly. I am putting down my papers. I have got a RJ job in a leading radio channel,' revealed Karthik.

Everyone was astonished, but Rini wasn't, as Karthik had already informed her about it. Jagan is out of words. He turned back and walked upstairs.

'Jagan, car parking is downstairs,' stopped Karthik.

'No, there is a bed available near Vinoth's dad. I can't take it anymore'

'Imagine what if you come to know about Aysha and Chocku in love,' Rini spilled the beans.

The brains of everyone froze and now they are in a situation to take any surprises. They wouldn't be surprised even if Mandhiravalli allowed for a team visit inside the ICU. Chocku acted like looking at his phone and Aysha not knowing how to react, compressed all sorts of expressions she had learnt in Bharatanatyam into one.

'How many secrets can I hold? I will get heart attack,' Rini scratched her head looking at Aysha.

'The heart is over here,' Karthik gestured to Rini by placing the hand on his chest. 'And not on head,' by scratching his head

'Shit. All my efforts have gone waste,' worried Chocku by seeing the phone.

'Aysha he is referring to falling in love with you,' kidded Karthik.

'Is it true?' asked Aysha.

'No. IT declaration date has been extended,' infuriated Chocku.

*

CHAPTER 10 – FAREWELL AND FRESHERS

After 2 months, Vinoth came to office as his father underwent bypass surgery. He took care of him until he recovered. Once he arrived, he sent his resignation mail to Jagan as informed earlier to him. Post reading the resignation mail, Jagan pinged Vinoth to come to his room.

'How is your dad now, Vinoth?'

'Getting better. He has almost recovered Jagan. Last 2 months have been very tough for us. He was suffering a lot due to surgery. Now he is on medication and the doctor has advised to follow a strict diet and go for a walk every day.'

'Good. I go jogging every day.'

'I sprint every day,'

Both compete with each other.

'I go for a long drive. Good for mental health.'

'Once I receive the PF, I may go on the flight,' and both laughed.

'We have hired two freshers. We somehow managed to find a replacement for you and Karthik. Kavita led the team well in your absence, but still there are some gaps to bridge which you can train her during your notice period. And our team will miss you and I will personally miss you.'

'Of course, me too Jagan,' and both paused for a moment.

'Okay. Rest I will give a speech about you during your farewell,' laughed Jagan.

'No, that would be too much.'

'No. You too, prepare a speech about me.'

'Sure Jagan,' nodded Vinoth.

'Come on. Stop nodding your head to everything I say. I was just kidding man. Also, today is the first day for freshers. Bring the team to the meeting room, we shall have a formal introduction.'

Everyone assembled in the conference room and Jagan was excited to introduce the new members to the team.

'Hi team, so the purpose of this meeting is to welcome our new members to the team. This is Balakumar, from Coimbatore.

He carries a smile throughout as if acting in a coffee ad. His body looks like a round glass bottle filled with coffee powder. If his head is the earth, belly is the moon and leg is the sun. When he looks down at his feet, a solar eclipse takes place in his body. The moon hides the sun.

Not knowing how to respond and get introduce himself to the team, he shook his hand only with Karthik and went back to his original position out of nervousness. And then he sensed that he should have shaken his hands with everyone. He again came forward and shook his hand with everyone going around. It looked awkward, but the teammates didn't want to embarrass him on his first day, so they responded to him casually.

'Hi madam, he shook his hand with Kavita, but she gestured by bowing down without uttering a word, instead 'Hi I am Kavita,' replied Aysha.'

'But what's her name?'

'Kavita.'

'Oh! Two Kavitas? '

'No, I am Aysha. She is Kavita. She is in a vow of silence.

'Oh! Okay madam.'

Jagan spoke in the local language Tamil as Balakumar wasn't effective in English communication.

Teammates

'Bala you needn't refer to me as sir and madam. Just call by their first name. Had Thiruvalluvar worked in IT, he would say *Call me valluvar, thiru is not required,*' Jagan enjoyed himself.

'Can you speak in English? I can't understand anything,' raised a stern voice.

'Ha Ha sure. I just forgot about you. So, he is Tanmoy Porel from Kolkata. North India.'

'Kolkata is in West Bengal, East India,' his words slit the throat of Jagan.

Teammates smirked and Jagan managed by sheepishly smiling.

Tanmoy is now the tallest member of the team, clean shaven and appears as if his arms, legs, face etc were made with rectangles yet hefty as well. His intense eyes look through a thick black frame spectacle as if it is to reduce the severity of his stare.

Meanwhile Rini, 'West Bengal should be a part of West India, right?' she asked Chocku and he facepalmed.

*

Karthik went through the relieving procedure by getting signatures from concerned departments and finally came to Jagan.

'So, when are you joining the channel?' received the paper from Karthik with a smiling face.

'Next week is the joining date.'

'Fine. Let me know the show timing. I will call and request my favourite song.'

'Not sure whether they would have such old songs in their list.'

'I still haven't signed your papers,' adjusted his spectacle.

'Sir, I am so excited to get a call from you. I am your big fan sir. I will play any song you wish. The whole show i will run the playlist of Jagan's favourites.'

'Ha-ha! You have chosen the right decision,' Jagan complimented and then signed the sheet.

*

Vinoth gave KT (Knowledge transfer) to the newly joined members, in the presence of the old members.

'So, this is our process. Do you have any doubts?'

'Oh, is this our process?' wondered Rini.

'I will go through the process and ask if I have any doubts,' said Tanmoy.

'I understood the process Vinoth, but what is KT? When will I get it?' asked Bala with high confidence.

The teammates laughed seeing his innocence

'While leaving the hall they will pin the KT Chocolate in the visiting card and give it to you,' kidded Karthik.

'Hey stop kidding. KT means Knowledge transfer. It's nothing but sharing information. What just happened now is KT,' explained Vinoth.

'Oh Okay,' laughed at himself and everyone giggled along with him.

'Ipadi sirikirangalae, Ivangaloda first day pathi sollatuma?', blackmailed Vinoth

'No,' pleaded all the old teammates.

'English Please!' commanded Tanmoy.

'I was saying, shall I talk about my experience with these old members on their first day?' he translated

'Yes, go on,' as if the mind failed to execute the smile command.

'4 years back, I had a discussion with Rini, Karthik and Aysha regarding their training period,'

Their mind rewinded 4 years back as Vinoth explained the moment.

'So, how did the training period go?' enquired Vinoth.

'It was fun. We went on a batch trip during weekends. Boat riding, beach, Mahabalipuram, Planetarium,' listed Rini

Pondicherry,' said Karthik.

'Shopping mall,' added Aysha.

'Contribution from everyone. Good teamwork,' mocked sarcastically. 'I meant what languages did you learn in your training period?'

'Visual Basic, PYTHON, SQL, HTML, XML C,' listed Aysha.

'C++,' added Rini.

'JAVA,' added Karthik.

'JAVA script,' Rini added again.

After deep thinking, 'R,' said Aysha.

'R++?' questioned Vinoth looking at Rini.

'Yes. I was about to say that.'

'Had she said terminator, you would have said terminator 2,' stared at her. 'What about DOTNET guys?'

Everyone nodded their head somewhere between Yes and No.

'So how much do you rate yourself in DOTNET?'

'70 out of 100,' rated Aysha.

'2.5 star,' rated Karthik.

'This is not a movie review. She told me out of 100, so stick to that.'

'Okay 50.'

'2.5,' said Rini.

'Pchh! I just said, please tell me out of 100.'

'Yeah 2.5.'

'Oh! I like your honest answer. No problem. We can train you.'

'Will you put me back in the training period,' came forward in curiosity.

'Why? Is there any other place you are yet to visit?' questioned sarcastically.

'No, I miss my batchmates,' replied Rini to which Vinoth shook his head as he was able to see the future of the team ahead. While he was worried about the freshers, someone opened the door and they all turned to see Kavita in a sleeveless semi traditional yet fancy and colourful churidar with embroidered neckline. The top is contrasted aesthetically with a bright-coloured handloom Banarasi dupatta and silk churidar pants. She also wore big ear rings as if they were stretching to touch her shoulder. Her free hair was dropped in front, almost hiding half of her face. Karthik, Aysha and Rini gazed at her in awe.

'May I come in?'

'I have blocked this hall. This meeting will end in 10 mins,' replied Vinoth.

'Even I was blocked on Aug 6, but in a much bigger hall.'

'Oh yes!' exclaimed as he was reminded about her marriage. 'So, Kavita is getting married guys,' informed the freshers and welcomed her to come in.

'I am leaving a bit early for marriage purchases today. I am already late, so I had to interrupt to officially invite you all. Sorry for the inconvenience.'

'Is it just today you left early?' laughed Vinoth.

Kavita felt that's in bad taste to tell it in front of everyone, but ignored as she was in a good mood.

She took the invitation card and gave it to Vinoth. He received it and rubbed his fingers on the invitation to feel the texture of it. Rini pulled it from Vinoth even before the sense of touch reached his brain. Then the three freshers discuss among themself looking at the invitation.

'Invitation looks really cool. What is he doing?' asked Rini.

'He was working in IT, but now he has quit his job to try for UPSC exams.'

'That's so great of you to support him. Is it love marriage?' asked Aysha.

'Yeah,' winked Kavita and her long eyelashes wiped away the inhibitions they had with their senior teammate. Even before getting to know about her, all three were impressed and willing to befriend her.

The door opened again, 'I have booked this hall,' came a lifeless voice and all turned back to see Chocku.

He looked lean with little sign of a growing belly. The hair pattern indicated two arrow marks to the side of his forehead symbolising the area where the hair fall is going to take place.

'When are you going to book the marriage hall Chocku?' asked Vinoth.

'Booking a marriage hall isn't convenient like booking a hall in our office. These marriage halls don't have proper software to book online. Lots of opportunities to be tapped by the software industry.'

Rini and Karthik smirked by passing comments to each other about his weird behaviour.

'Stop it guys. He would feel bad if he comes to know that you are teasing him,' whispered Aysha.

'Why do you literally take my question?' Vinoth shook his head. 'I indirectly meant when is your marriage and when are you going to give us your marriage invitation?' replied Vinoth to Chocku

'Get ready to receive the invitation next month,' told with sheer confidence.

*

Back to the present, and all laugh out loud about Chocku still being unmarried.

'How many kids do you have, Chocku bro?' asked Bala.

'Get ready to receive the invitation next month,' replied Chocku.

'Are you still unmarried?' astonished Bala.

'This time next month for sure,' looked at Aysha romantically.

'Ohh!' shouted everyone.

'Why? What Oh?' confused Tanmoy.

'Tanmoy u don't understand tamil. U don't understand this also vah?' teased Balakumar by rolling his eyes towards Aysha and Chocku To and Fro.

'Ahh! now I get it.'

'Next month is too early. I need some more time,' said Aysha.

'Next month invitation kudukadhu,' teased Tanmoy in broken tamil meaning *You are not going to give the invitation next month too.*

'Varadhu da. Aena naan unaku kudukamaten,' Chocku replied in a friendly tone in Tamil which meant 'Yes, because I will not give it to you.'

Rini came forward to explain it to Tanmoy.

'No need of explanation. I can understand the pain of a single's emotion,' said Tanmoy and even Chocku laughed along with them.

'Why Kavita is not speaking?' enquired Tanmoy.

Bala who already had asked about it from others came forward and explained, 'I Know I will tell. Kavita kid no, he has constipation, so to go smoothly,'

Tanmoy closed his nose.

'She took mouna viradham, Mouth won't speak today. Prayer to God!' Bala looked up and joined his hands like praying

'Arey Yaar *(colloquial hindi word used when a person in anguish).* Your explanation is messier than the shit,' the team were in splits.

*

Karthik deep inside felt that he had a good relationship with Rini being around and mocking her, but never really had any serious conversation. Now when the time has come to move away, he was concerned about her, so he decided to express his thoughts.

'I will miss you a lot Rini.'

'Really? I hope you don't have a punchline if I reply *Miss you too.*'

'May be, I will literally punch you if you say that *You don't miss me.*

Laughed and said, 'I will miss you a lot too buddy' and they fist bump.

'I wanted to talk to you about something.'

'Even I had to talk to you about something. Okay farewell boy first.'

'As far as I have known you, professionally you too aren't much interested in IT like me. The difference is I tried hard to develop interest in this field, but you hardly cared about it. What do you really have in your mind?'

'Not thinking much about it. Just going with the flow.'

'I am damn sure this flow will lead towards firing.'

'So what? Then I will be a free bird.'

'Free bird? You will fly directly to the bird hunter to get fired again,' teased Karthik and she tapped on his shoulder playfully.

'But jokes apart, you should figure out something, but not sure what,' he desperately tried to suggest something, but he couldn't.

'Okay now it's my turn to talk.'

'Fine. Go on.'

'People like you have made me realise that I should do something that satisfies my soul and then finally I did find. I have applied for a Kindergarten teacher course. The course will start in a month and I will be attending classes every weekend.'

'Hey really! *This can be the best farewell gift,*' expressed like a kid opening the gift box.

'I genuinely feel my soul satisfaction lies with those pure souls. And I even have set a target to achieve in my life which is unlike me. I wanted to teach 10000 kids in my life by taking classes, tuition, conducting workshops and any other possible means,' with so much curiosity in face.

'I feel so right about this decision. Now when I think about your nature and having known you well, this profession would fit the puzzle perfectly. I am so happy for you.'

'Your words do give me more confidence. In fact, I wanted to talk to you about this before, but I myself wasn't sure how serious I am about this decision. It took me a lot of time for me to feel right about it. I have told only to you and will convey to Aysha tonight probably. Once I complete the course and get the job, that's when I can reveal it to our teammates.'

'Fine, but my only concern is..,' hesitated Karthik.

'What? Please feel free to tell me.'

'Going by your knowledge in mathematics, I wonder how you will keep track of 10000 kids?', teased Karthik.

*

'Guys, it's time for Karthik's farewell,' announced Vinoth and all gathered in the conference room.

Jagan began his typical IT farewell speech, 'He has been an outstanding employee of the office from the date he joined. It is his fortune that he got a new opportunity to pursue his passion, however it is our misfortune that we are missing a nice colleague forever. Being the Manager, I would like to say something here about him.

The teammates yawned.

'He has made the functioning more organised and less challenging by implementing more strategic plans which we generally thought impossible to implement.'

The teammates looked at Karthik in awe like 'Did you?'

'Is he thinking it's Aysha's farewell?' whispered Karthik.

'We really will miss you very much, especially for making us laugh daily. It is very difficult for us to give farewell to you and replace you with another colleague.'

Tanmoy and Balakumar looked at each other and shook their heads in disappointment as they came as replacement for Karthik and Vinoth.

'On behalf of everyone, I wish you good luck and..'

'Yayyy!' screamed Kavita.

'Payan ai poitana?' asked Aysha as if she found gold in her backyard.

'Tanmoy, she is asking whether Kavita's kid is going shit smoothly,' translated Bala.

'No. My husband has got 9th rank in UPSC exams,' informed Kavita excitedly. Had there been a metrics to calculate happiness, she would have got 9th rank in the world.

Everyone became elated and congratulated her.

'This is the best gift I can get for my farewell,' exclaimed Karthik and shook hands with Kavita. A hand tapped him from behind and he turned around to notice Rini.

She asked softly yet in a deadly tone, 'How many best gifts have you received sir?' raised one of her sharp eyebrows that seemed like a sword being pulled out from a case.

Ahem! Had I told them it's the second-best gift, then I would have to reveal the best gift which is your secret,' managed playfully.

'So, your kid hasn't shit yet?' asked Chocku as if he was among the least 10 ranks in happiness index.

'Idiot. I took a vow of silence for my husband's UPSC result only.'

'I am yet to finish my farewell speech,' announced Jagan.

'I think you should start the farewell speech for me now, so that it will end on my farewell day,' teased Vinoth.

'Ha-ha! Fine, let's start the cake cutting then,' gave way for the teammates to celebrate the occasion.

'Come Kavita, let's cut the cake together,' invited Karthik and they cut the cake together.

'Everyone, please ensure you eat every bit of it,' said Kavita.

'Yes, else Kavita will parcel it to her home,' kidded Rini.

*

Last few minutes left for Karthik to leave the office and it hurt him as he imagined that he is not going to come back to office tomorrow. Rini knew he was upset and planned to freshen him up, literally. She called Aysha and Kavita to Karthik's place.

'Let's do make over like a girl and make his day special,' said Rini.

Karthik panicked at first, but later accepted as this is the last wish from his lovely teammates.

They collected all their cosmetic items and placed them on the table. The bay was roaring with fun and as Jagan crossed the bay, they abruptly reduced the noise. He noticed the teammates applying cosmetics on Karthik.

'Put some mascara too,' commented Jagan while walking to his room.

As he walked, he imagined his fresher days, when his teammates turned him into a girl by intertwining his long silky hair on both the sides and applying cosmetics on his face. He felt shy and overwhelmed as the girls from other cubicles smiled at him.

He felt nostalgic, smiled to himself and then walked back to the bay to announce 'I know it's too late, but let's celebrate this moment. Why not go out for dinner tonight? The treat is on me.'

Everyone agreed, but Kavita hesitated as her husband would come to pick up. Jagan, realised even before she raised a concern.

'Kavita, your husband would come to pick you up, right? It would be great if your husband and kid join us today. Our teammates would love to host him on this happy occasion.'

'Sure Jagan. I will check with him and confirm right away'. She then made a call to her husband and confirmed his presence for dinner.

The time was 7 pm and they started to leave for dinner. Everyone kept access and left the ODC one by one. Karthik waited in the cubicle while others were leaving. He then enacted like walking towards the door and then ran back once they left, opened his bag and hid the gifts in each of their seats, so that they will be surprised the next morning.

Finally, he left the bay and walked towards the door only to be surprised. He made a call to Rini.

'Rini, I am stuck here. I have submitted my access card. Bail me out please.'

All the teammates heard Rini talking with him, 'Are you caught inside? I am coming now,' laughed Rini and others were in splits.

'He can't escape from IT,' commented Vinoth.

Karthik disconnected the phone and waited for Rini to come. Heard a voice 'Karthik Sir' and he turned to find the security anna Velumani.

'Anna.'

Teammates

'Sir. Why are you waiting near the door? Didn't you bring the access card today?'

'Anna,' exclaimed Karthik. 'I am very glad that I saw you now. Today is my last day anna. I will be joining the radio channel next week as I told you earlier. Hereafter, you can hear my show durimng your night shift and hope I entertain you.,' smiled Karthik.

"Happy for you Sir. All the best", blessed him wholeheartedly by placing his hand on his head and Karthik got his contact number.

Security swiped the access and the glass door slide opened. He left with a heavy heart and met Rini midway. They both joined their teammates at downstairs. Rini conveyed to them that the security had bailed him out.

'That's his best gift ever,' teased Kavita and that cracked up the teammates. As their laugh subsided, Jagan informed them, 'Guys next week I will be going to meet the Coimbatore team.'

'This is the best gift you can give your teammates,' commented Karthik

'Uff! These employees after they put down their papers,' sighed Jagan and the teammates cracked up. The fun continued with them in a never ending loop without a 'break' statement.

*

Made in the USA
Monee, IL
03 May 2026

49438457R00115